Ambrose / Harris

TYPOGRAPHY

n. the arrangement,
style and appearance of
type and typefaces

AVA Publishing SA
Switzerland

An AVA Book
Published by AVA Publishing SA
Chemin de la Joliette 2, Case postale 96
1000 Lausanne 6, Switzerland
Tel: +41 786 005 109 Email: enquiries@avabooks.ch

Distributed by Thames & Hudson (ex-North America)
181a High Holborn, London WC1V 7QX, United Kingdom
Tel: +44 20 7845 5000 Fax: +44 20 7845 5055
Email: sales@thameshudson.co.uk
www.thamesandhudson.com

For distribution in the USA and Canada please contact:
English Language Support Office
AVA Publishing (UK) Ltd.
Tel: +44 1903 204 455 Email: sales@avabooks.co.uk

English Language Support Office
AVA Publishing (UK) Ltd.
Tel: +44 1903 204 455 Email: enquiries@avabooks.co.uk

ISBN 2-88479-064-0
10 9 8 7 6 5 4 3 2 1

Design and text by Gavin Ambrose and Paul Harris
Original photography by Xavier Young – www.xavieryoung.co.uk
Image on page 150 by Rocco Redondo
Images on page 57 and page 89 by Richard Learoyd
Original book and series concept devised by Natalia Price-Cabrera

Production and separations by AVA Book Production Pte. Ltd., Singapore
Tel: +65 6334 8173 Fax: +65 6334 0752 Email: production@avabooks.com.sg

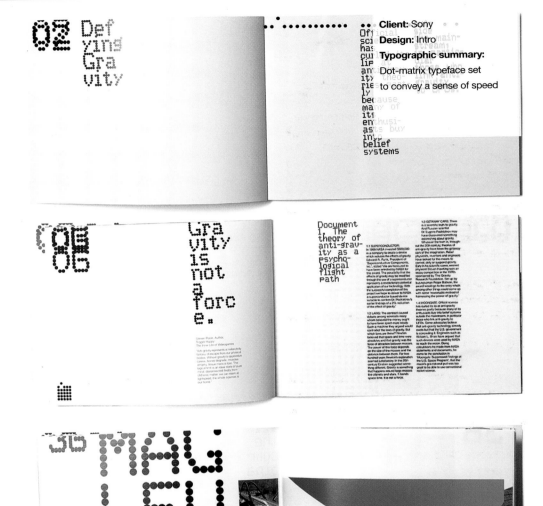

Client: Sony

Design: Intro

Typographic summary:
Dot-matrix typeface set to convey a sense of speed

Defying Gravity

This booklet, created by Intro design studio, accompanied the launch of *Wipeout Fusion*; *a* game for Sony's Playstation 2. The dot-matrix typeface used is erratically typeset and the use of overprinting, bleeds and different column configurations all combine to reflect the frenetic sense of movement and speed that the game has.

Contents

Why Not Associates

Still Waters Run Deep

Studio Myerscough

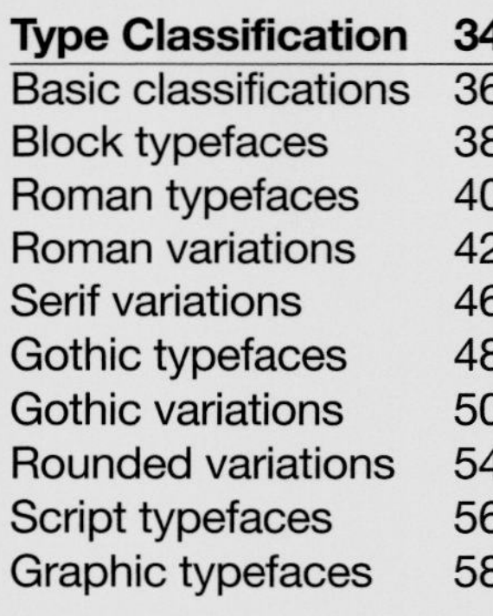

3 Deep Design

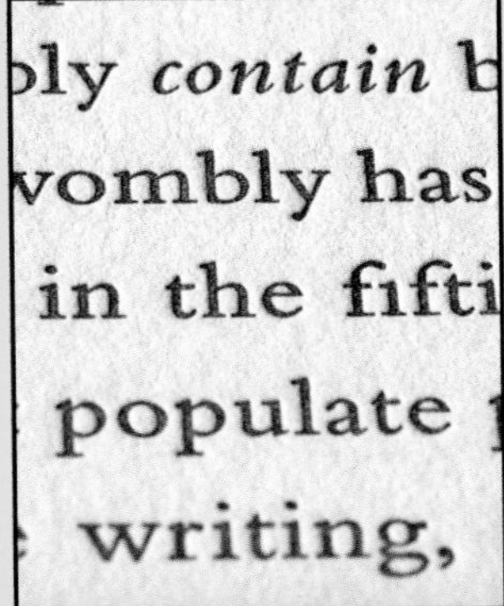

Bruce Mau Design

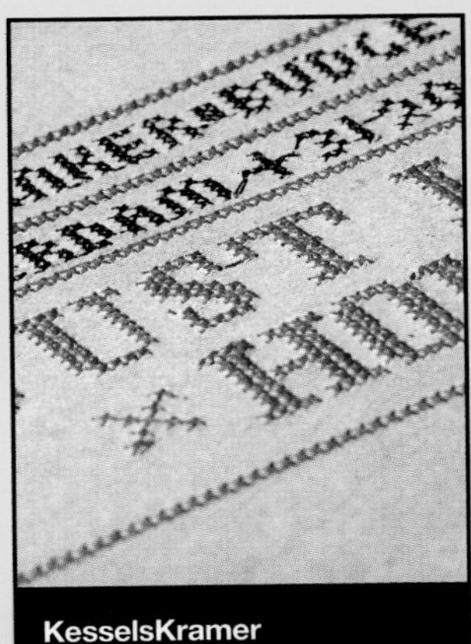
KesselsKramer

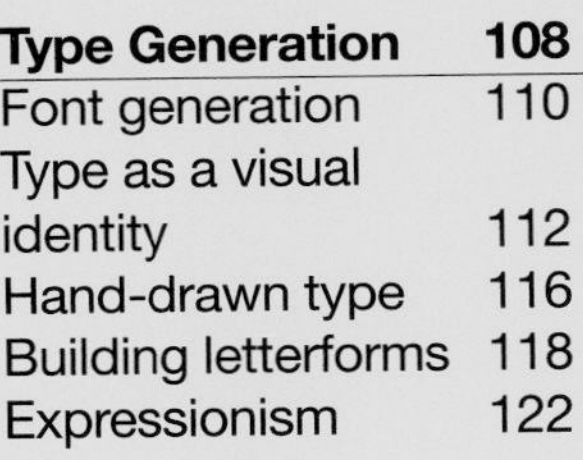

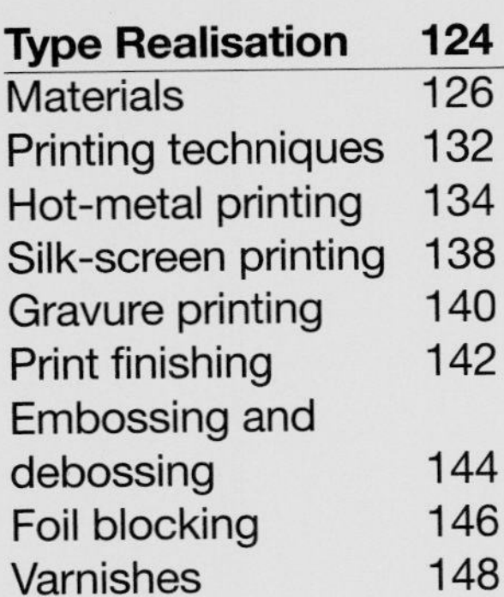

Introduction

Typography is the means by which a written idea is given a visual form. Due to the volume and variety of typefaces available, the selection of the components of this visual form can dramatically affect the readability of the idea and a reader's feelings towards it. Typography is one of the most influential elements on the character and emotional quality of a design. It can produce a neutral effect or rouse the passions, it can symbolise artistic, political or philosophical movements, or it can express the personality of an individual or organisation.

Typefaces vary from clear and distinguishable letterforms that flow easily before the eye, and so are suitable for extended blocks of text, to those more dramatic and eye-catching typefaces that grab attention and so are used in headlines and advertisements.

Typography is anything but static and continues to evolve. Many typefaces in current use find their foundations in designs created during earlier historical epochs. The fledgling printing industry in the 15th century established Roman capitals and Carolingian minuscules, these were further developed during the reign of Charlemagne as standard letterforms and many are still widely used today.

Looking at Type

Definitions of some of the most common typographical terms are explained, providing a basic understanding of letterforms and typography. Although often named after superseded technologies, these terms are still in general use and particularly relevant.

Type Classification

A sound understanding of how typefaces are classified is crucial for the modern designer. It is necessary in order to appreciate the historical relevance of type and to recognise the nuances of available type forms.

Setting Type

Exploring how type can be measured and manipulated facilitates a level of design control and finesse. Basic techniques and structures are explained to help a designer use type effectively.

Type Generation

Many pieces of work require bespoke typographical solutions, often these will include the adjustment of existing typefaces or the generation of new ones.

Type Realisation

The realisation or placement of type can dramatically add to the effectiveness and intensity of a design. Considerations of paper stocks and printing techniques can profoundly enhance a finished design and the examples contained within this section serve to demonstrate this.

Type in Practice

In this concluding section we explore some of the more unusual requirements and demands made of typography. The basic understandings discussed in previous sections serve to underpin these more experimental realisations.

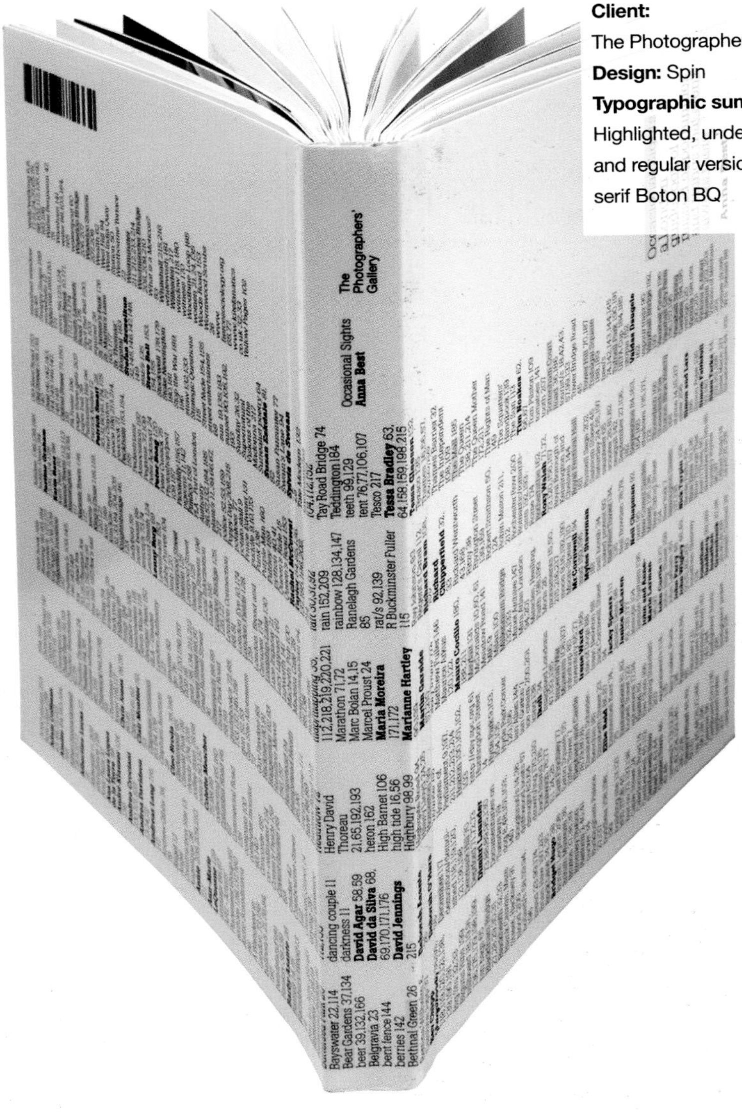

Client:
The Photographers' Gallery
Design: Spin
Typographic summary:
Highlighted, underlined, bold and regular versions of slab serif Boton BQ

Occasional Sights

Occasional Sights is a guidebook to London created by artist Anna Best, which explores missed opportunities and things that do not really exist in the UK capital. The design by Spin features a cover that also serves as a complete index to the book's contents; something more commonly contained within the closing pages of a publication. The index uses highlighted, underlined, bold and regular versions of Boton BQ, an Egyptian slab-serif typeface. This typeface closely mimics the character impressions made by a typewriter and is traditionally used to compensate for coarse paper stocks and low-grade printing.

This book introduces different aspects of typographical design via dedicated chapters for each topic. Each chapter provides numerous examples of creative use of typography in design from leading contemporary design studios, annotated to explain the reasons behind the design choices made.

Key design principles are isolated so that the reader can see how they are applied in practice.

Clear navigation
Each chapter entry has a clear strapline to allow readers to quickly locate areas of interest.

Background information
Summarised information accompanies each example.

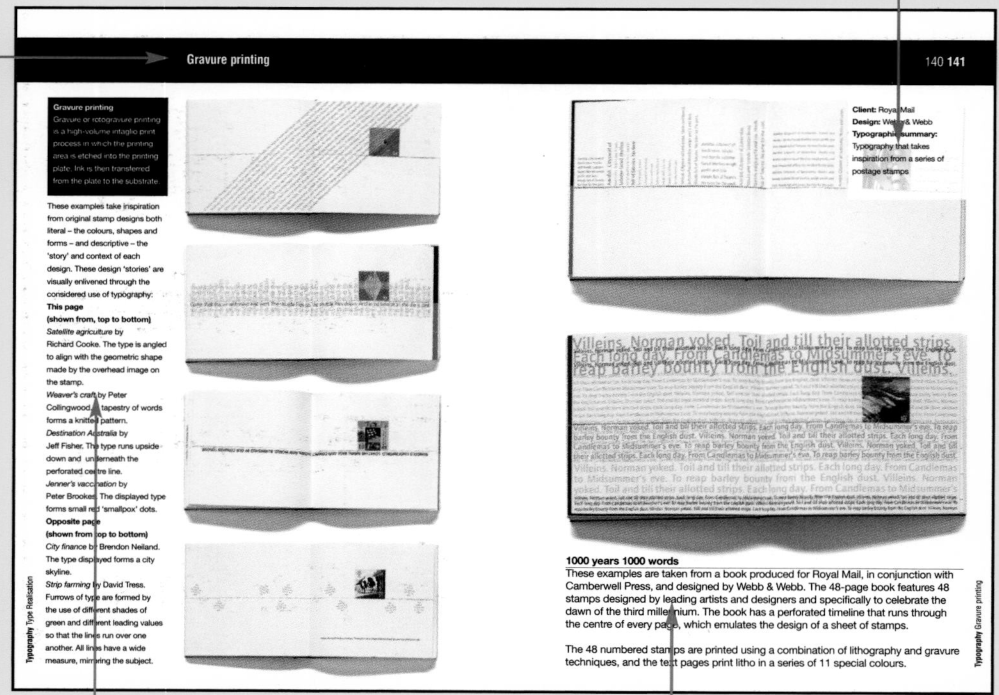

Gravure printing 140 141

Gravure printing
Gravure or rotogravure printing is a high-volume intaglio print process in which the printing area is etched into the printing plate. Ink is then transferred from the plate to the substrate.

These examples take inspiration from original stamp designs both literal – the colours, shapes and forms – and descriptive – the 'story' and context of each design. These design 'stories' are visually enlivened through the considered use of typography:
This page
(shown from, top to bottom)
Satellite agriculture by Richard Cooke. The type is angled to align with the geometric shape made by the overhead image on the stamp.
Weaver's craft by Peter Collingwood. A tapestry of words forms a knitted pattern.
Destination Australia by Jeff Fisher. The type runs upside down and underneath the perforated centre line.
Jenner's vaccination by Peter Brookes. The displayed type forms small red 'smallpox' dots.
Opposite page
(shown from top to bottom)
City finance by Brendon Neiland. The type displayed forms a city skyline.
Strip farming by David Tress. Furrows of type are formed by the use of different shades of green and different leading values so that the lines run over one another. All lines have a wide measure, mirroring the subject.

Client: Royal Mail
Design: Webb & Webb
Typographic summary:
Typography that takes inspiration from a series of postage stamps

1000 years 1000 words
These examples are taken from a book produced for Royal Mail, in conjunction with Camberwell Press, and designed by Webb & Webb. The 48-page book features 48 stamps designed by leading artists and designers and specifically to celebrate the dawn of the third millennium. The book has a perforated timeline that runs through the centre of every page, which emulates the design of a sheet of stamps.

The 48 numbered stamps are printed using a combination of lithography and gravure techniques, and the text pages print litho in a series of 11 special colours.

Typography Type Realisation

Typography Gravure printing

Additional information
Supporting information accompanies diagrams and examples, putting the work into context.

Explanatory texts
Key points are introduced and simply explained.

Introductions
Special section introductions outline basic concepts that are to be discussed.

Written explanations
Key points are explained within the context of an example project.

Examples
Commercial projects from contemporary designers bring the principles under discussion to life.

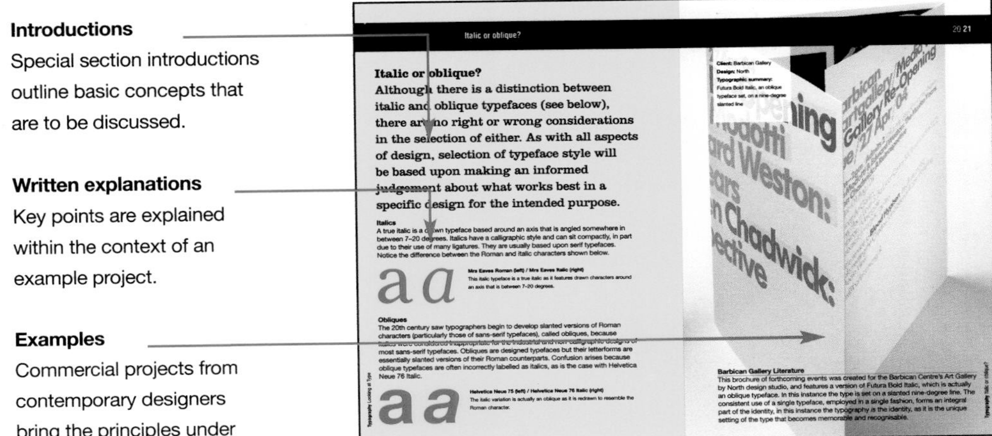
Italic or oblique?

20 21

Italic or oblique?
Although there is a distinction between italic and oblique typefaces (see below), there are no right or wrong considerations in the selection of either. As with all aspects of design, selection of typeface style will be based upon making an informed judgement about what works best in a specific design for the intended purpose.

Italics
A true italic is a drawn typeface based around an axis that is angled somewhere in between 7–20 degrees. Italics have a calligraphic style and can sit compactly, in part due to their use of many ligatures. They are usually based upon serif typefaces. Notice the difference between the Roman and italic characters shown below.

a *a*

Mrs Eaves Roman (left) / Mrs Eaves Italic (right)
This italic typeface is a true italic as it features drawn characters around an axis that is between 7–20 degrees.

Obliques
The 20th century saw typographers begin to develop slanted versions of Roman characters (particularly those of sans-serif typefaces), called obliques, because italics were considered inappropriate for the industrial and non-calligraphic designs of most sans-serif typefaces. Obliques are designed typefaces but their letterforms are essentially slanted versions of their Roman counterparts. Confusion arises because oblique typefaces are often incorrectly labelled as italics, as is the case with Helvetica Neue 76 Italic.

a *a*

Helvetica Neue 75 (left) / Helvetica Neue 76 Italic (right)
The italic variation is actually an oblique as it is redrawn to resemble the Roman character.

Typography Looking at Type

Client: Barbican Gallery
Design: North
Typographic summary:
Futura Bold Italic, an oblique typeface set, on a nine-degree slanted line

Barbican Gallery Literature
This brochure of forthcoming events was created for the Barbican Centre's Art Gallery by North design studio, and features a version of Futura Bold Italic, which is actually an oblique typeface. In this instance the type is set on a slanted nine-degree line. The consistent use of a single typeface, employed in a single fashion, forms an integral part of the identity, in this instance the typography *is* the identity, as it is the unique setting of the type that becomes memorable and recognisable.

Typography Italic or oblique?

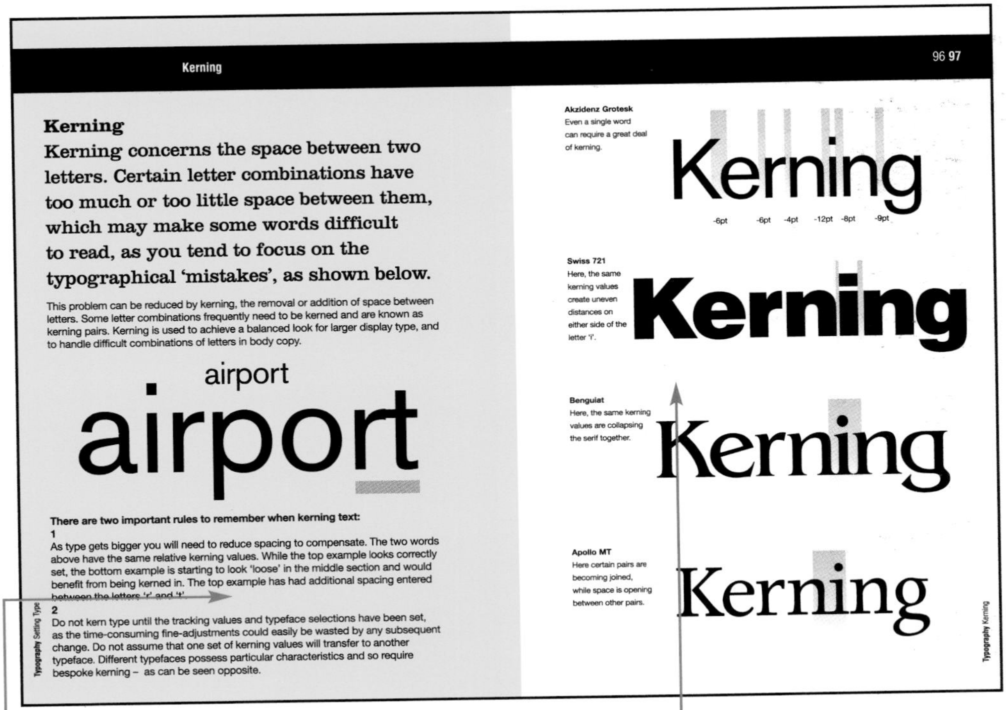

Kerning

96 97

Kerning
Kerning concerns the space between two letters. Certain letter combinations have too much or too little space between them, which may make some words difficult to read, as you tend to focus on the typographical 'mistakes', as shown below.

This problem can be reduced by kerning, the removal or addition of space between letters. Some letter combinations frequently need to be kerned and are known as kerning pairs. Kerning is used to achieve a balanced look for larger display type, and to handle difficult combinations of letters in body copy.

airport

airport

There are two important rules to remember when kerning text:

1
As type gets bigger you will need to reduce spacing to compensate. The two words above have the same relative kerning values. While the top example looks correctly set, the bottom example is starting to look 'loose' in the middle section and would benefit from being kerned in. The top example has had additional spacing entered between the letters 'r' and 't'.

2
Do not kern type until the tracking values and typeface selections have been set, as the time-consuming fine-adjustments could easily be wasted by any subsequent change. Do not assume that one set of kerning values will transfer to another typeface. Different typefaces possess particular characteristics and so require bespoke kerning – as can be seen opposite.

Typography Setting Type

Akzidenz Grotesk
Even a single word can require a great deal of kerning.

Kerning

-6pt -6pt -4pt -12pt -8pt -9pt

Swiss 721
Here, the same kerning values create uneven distances on either side of the letter 'i'.

Kerning

Benguiat
Here, the same kerning values are collapsing the serif together.

Kerning

Apollo MT
Here certain pairs are becoming joined, while space is opening between other pairs.

Kerning

Typography Kerning

Technical information
Typographic theory and terminology is decoded to foster greater understanding of typographic concepts.

Diagrams
Diagrams add meaning to the theory by showing it in action.

Client: Royal Academy of Arts
Design: Why Not Associates
Typographic summary:
Logotype with infilled counters, specifically designed for the exhibition's promotional material

ROYAL ACADEMY OF ARTS
PICCADILLY W1

APOCALYPSE
BEAUTY AND HORROR IN CONTEMPORARY ART

23 SEPTEMBER-15 DECEMBER 2000
DAILY 10am-6pm FRIDAYS UNTIL 8.30pm
www.royalacademy.org.uk

Looking at Type

Within its broad parameters typography contains a wealth of specialised terminology, which designers and printers use when examining or describing typefaces and their associated characteristics. Whilst each term has a specific meaning, some of these definitions have become distorted over time or otherwise altered by common usage, and this can result in confusion. For example, many people incorrectly refer to 'obliques' as 'italics' simply because they both slant.

Many of these terms, such as 'leading' or 'em rule', originate from the hot-metal printing industry. Until the explosive impact of information technology, seen in recent times, this industry was the bastion of typography. Similarly a number of terms – including the names given to individual parts of a single character – date back even further and find their origins in stonemasonry.

This chapter introduces and defines some of the most common typographical terms used when looking at and describing a typeface, as well as its synonyms and alternative, distorted uses.

An understanding of the terminology contained within this volume will not only enable you to discuss, specify and communicate typographic requirements with clients, designers and industry professionals, but will also result in a deeper understanding of the subject.

'We should welcome typographic variety as the natural consequence of human creativity.'
Sebastian Carter

Apocalypse (left)

This poster was created for the *Apocalypse* show at the Royal Academy of Arts in London. Beauty and horror are visually expressed via the harsh juxtaposition of the apocalyptic typography, which overlays and cuts into the serene image. The simple removal of the counters from the letters serves to dehumanise them, and implies sinister overtones. The typography appears in three distinct blocks that are centred on the page, creating a simple hierarchy of information – who, what and when. This text placement, often considered traditional, is also subverted by the apocalyptic title.

Where type is used

Type is everywhere. It is on almost everything we buy, on the pages of books and magazines, on walls, floors and street signs. As the examples here demonstrate, there are many typeface varieties and each possesses a distinct personality. Some typefaces are formal and convey a sense of authority, while others are more relaxed and appear to be less structured. Typeface usage can therefore tell a reader as much about the originator of the communication as the message itself.

If rendered sympathetically, a hand-drawn board outside a restaurant may imply the menu changes regularly. However, if crudely presented, the board may give the impression that preparation at the venue is sloppy; not a positive message for a restaurant! Type is everywhere and how it is set affects how its message is read, as this can be reinforced or contradicted by the typeface that is used to present it.

Type tells us what to do…

…and what not to do.

Type can have character…

... or be utilitarian...

...or austere.

Type can be permanent...

...or temporary.

Type can help us find our way...

...or be confusing.

Type can make one thing...

...different from another.

Type can be informal...

...or formal.

Type can be festive and shout...

...or be sad.

Type can be crude...

...or anarchic...

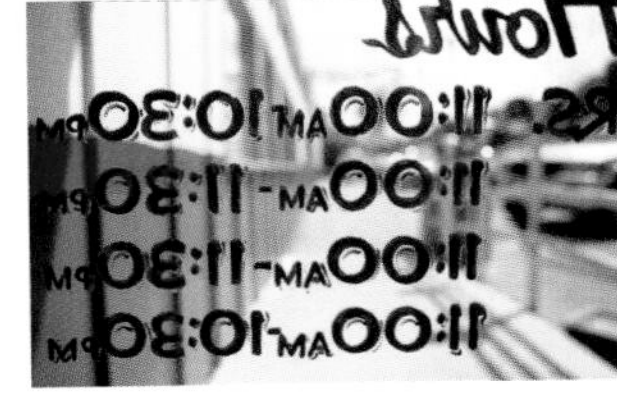

...but it is everywhere.

What is type?

Typographer Eric Gill noted that 'letters are things, they are not pictures of things'. Individual letters, when arranged in a particular way, represent the sounds of a spoken language and visually express ideas in such a way that another person can understand them in the manner intended.

Typography concerns the setting of letters within a design, usually for the purposes of printing. The variety of typefaces and the different ways in which typefaces can be used within a design, can enhance or alter the meaning of the very words that the type is used to create. The style in which letters are formed and presented alters our perceptions of the ideas they are portraying, as the examples below demonstrate.

Modern

Foundry Gridnik

The gridded lines pay homage to a font designed by Wim Crowel in the late 1960s that was never released. The even weight, angular structure and 'visible' grid-lines result in a modern, almost futuristic typeface.

Handwritten

Zapf Chancery

In contrast Hermann Zapf's distinctive calligraphic typeface is based on chancery handwriting, a style developed during the Italian Renaissance and used by scribes.

Ornate

Kuenstler Script

Reminiscent of intricate handwriting, Kuenstler Script sacrifices a degree of legibility in favour of overall flair.

Simple

Gill Sans

Originally produced for the London & North Eastern Railway, here the emphasis is on legibility.

Futuristic

Eurostile

Aldo Novarese's seminal font reflects the optimism of 1950s' and 1960s' design.

Historical

Garamond

Evergreen font by Claude Garamond conveys a sense of classicism and historical importance.

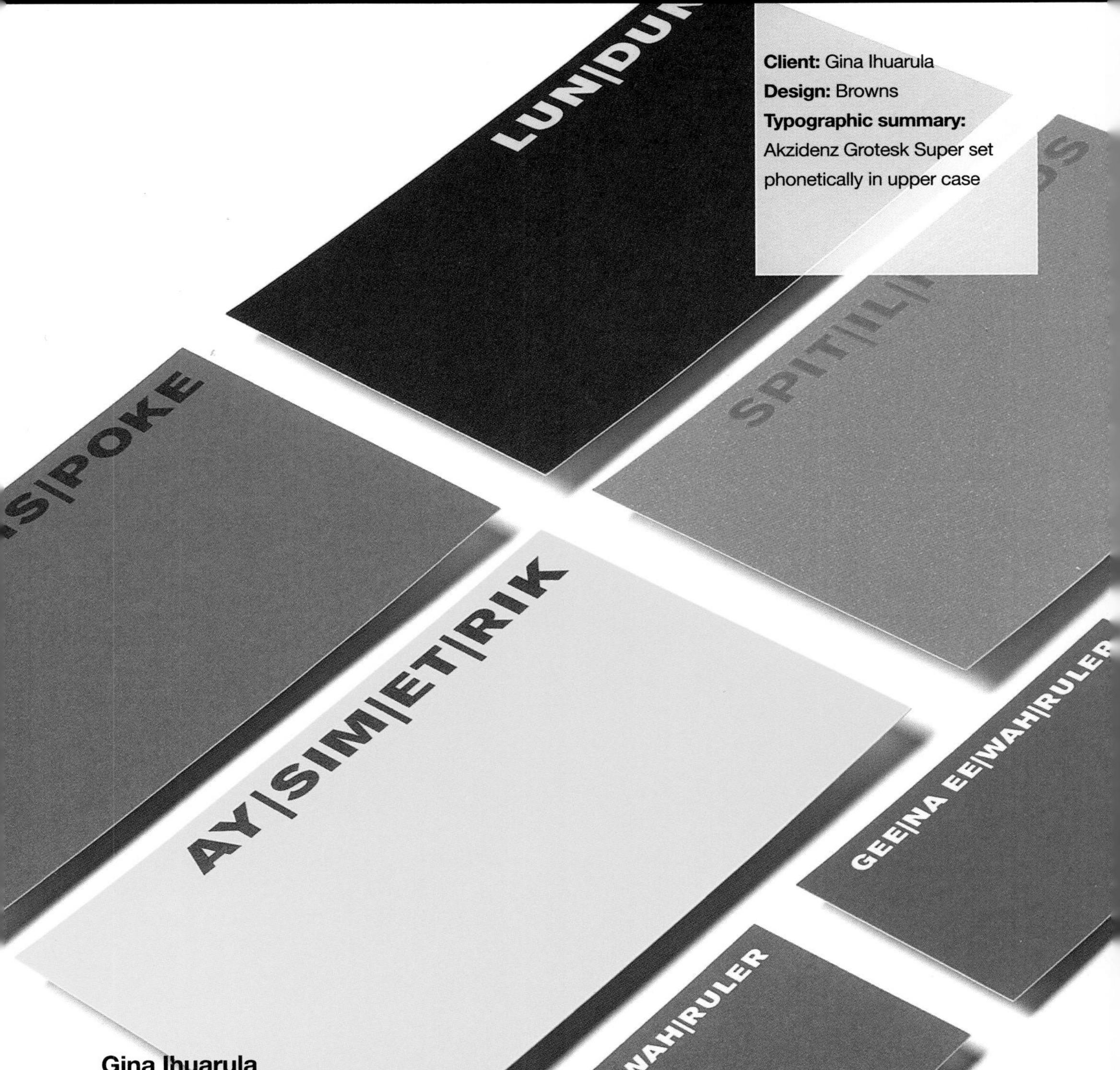

Client: Gina Ihuarula
Design: Browns
Typographic summary:
Akzidenz Grotesk Super set phonetically in upper case

Gina Ihuarula

This bold identity created for London fashion designer Gina Ihuarula demonstrates the power of type and colour. As the name 'Ihuarula' is difficult to pronounce, Browns employed a phonetic construction to inform people of its correct pronunciation, EE-WAH-RULER. The use of an upper case sans-serif typeface (Akzidenz Grotesk Super) adds authority and clarity to the text.

Pictured above are several applications from the identity created, which illustrate how the phonetic scheme was applied to those words that best relate to Gina Ihuarula's occupation as a fashion designer. Thus we have BIS-POKE (bespoke), LUN-DUN (London) and AY-SIM-ET-RIK (asymmetric).

Typefaces and fonts (or founts)

In common usage, the words 'typeface' and 'font' are used synonymously. In most cases there is no harm in doing so as such substitution is virtually universal and most people, including designers, would be hard pressed to state each word's 'correct' definition if asked. However, each term does possess separate and quite distinct meanings.

According to James Felici's *Complete Manual of Typography*, a typeface is a collection of characters, letters, numbers, symbols, punctuation (and so on), which have the same, distinct design. A font however, is the physical means of typeface production, be it the description of a typeface in computer code, lithographic film, metal or woodcut. Felici explains this distinction in simple terms, and describes the font as a cookie cutter and the typeface as the cookie produced from the cutter. When looking at a design, one can ask what typeface it uses or what font the type is set in, but strictly speaking, one cannot ask what font it uses.

Below left is the font (or cookie cutter), which is used to produce the typeface (or cookie), shown on the right.

Typeface

A typeface is a collection of characters, letters, numbers, symbols, punctuation (and so on), which have the same, distinct design.

Font (or fount)

A font (or fount) is the physical means used to create a typeface, be it computer code, lithographic film, metal or woodcut.

Typeface style

A typeface family contains the range of different character styles, which can be applied to the same basic Roman typeface.

This is illustrated below with the Helvetica Neue family. Roman is the basic cut and base style in which the majority of body text will be set. The other family members are variations of this and allow a designer greater flexibility to provide variation and emphasis, as and when required, to produce a more interesting and useful design, whilst preserving key typeface characteristics.

Roman

Helvetica Neue 55
Originates from inscriptions found on Roman monuments – some typefaces also carry a slightly lighter version called 'Book'.

Italic

Helvetica Neue 56
A version of the Roman cut that slopes to the right. Most typefaces have an italic version.

Condensed

Helvetica Condensed
Condensed is a narrower version of the Roman cut.

Extended

Helvetica Neue Extended
Extended is a wider version of the Roman cut.

Boldface

Helvetica Neue 75
Uses a wider stroke than Roman and is also called medium, semi-bold, black, super and poster.

Light or thin

Helvetica Neue 35
A variation of the Roman cut with a lighter stroke.

Client: Stroom
Design:
Faydherbe / De Vringer
Typographic summary:
Leviathan HTF black italic typeface, slashed words convey motion and immediacy

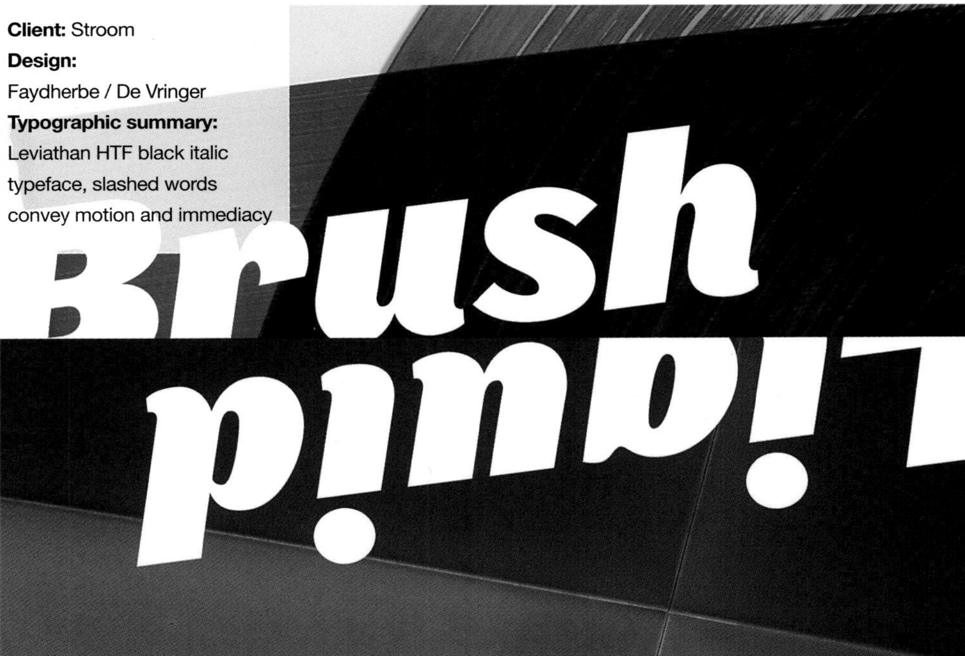

Toussaintkade 55

Deze voormalige broodjesfabriek wordt al meer dan tien jaar als expositieruimte gebruikt.
Het kunstenaarscollectief Quartair dat het pand beheert, gebruikt het in de zomer, Stroom hcbk organiseert in de wintermaanden tentoonstellingen, waarvoor met name Haagse kunstenaars worden uitgenodigd.

The Brush and the Liquid

Henk Hubenet en Mark de Weijer

De schilders Henk Hubenet en Mark de Weijer hebben elkaar leren kennen in een voormalig schoolgebouw, waar sinds 2000 de stichting Ruimtevaart is gevestigd.
Na verloop van tijd ontstond er een wederzijdse interesse in elkaars werk, dat op diverse punten overeenkomsten bleek te hebben.
Beide schilders hanteren modernistische uitgangspunten. Het onderwerp is de schilderkunst zelf waarbij de abstractie het resultaat is van een nauwgezette reeks van handelingen.
Van belang hierbij is de zintuiglijkheid van kleur, huid, schaal en proportie. De werken zijn echter onontkoombaar individueel.
Zo improviseert Henk Hubenet, op het scherpst van de snede, met vormstylering en kleurcombinaties.
Mark de Weijer past kleur- en materiaalexperimenten seriematig toe waarbij de reeks zowel een utilitaire als autonome waarde lijkt te representeren.

Ontwerp: Ben Faydherbe (Faydherbe/De Vringer)

Uitnodiging

Henk Hubenet en Mark de Weijer

The Brush and the Liquid
Schilderkunst in relatie tot Newton en Newman

Opening

donderdag 8 januari 2004, 17 uur

Toussaintkade 55, Den Haag
9 januari tm 8 februari 2004
woensdag tm zondag 12–17 uur

TPG Post
Port betaald
Port payé
Pays-Bas

s t r o o m

haags centrum voor beeldende kunst

spui 193-195
2511 bn den haag
telefoon 070 3658985

www.stroom.nl
e-mail: info@stroom.nl
fax 070 3617962

Stroom Invitation

This invitation for Stroom – a visual arts centre in the Netherlands – was created by Faydherbe / De Vringer and uses an italic typeface to convey the motion that one associates with the movement of a paintbrush. The words are slashed or truncated to suggest a sense of immediacy.

Italic or oblique?

Although there is a distinction between italic and oblique typefaces (see below), there are no right or wrong considerations in the selection of either. As with all aspects of design, selection of typeface style will be based upon making an informed judgement about what works best in a specific design for the intended purpose.

Italics

A true italic is a drawn typeface based around an axis that is angled somewhere in between 7–20 degrees. Italics have a calligraphic style and can sit compactly, in part due to their use of many ligatures. They are usually based upon serif typefaces. Notice the difference between the Roman and italic characters shown below.

Mrs Eaves Roman (left) / Mrs Eaves Italic (right)

This italic typeface is a true italic as it features drawn characters around an axis that is between 7–20 degrees.

Obliques

The 20th century saw typographers begin to develop slanted versions of Roman characters (particularly those of sans-serif typefaces), called obliques, because italics were considered inappropriate for the industrial and non-calligraphic designs of most sans-serif typefaces. Obliques are designed typefaces but their letterforms are essentially slanted versions of their Roman counterparts. Confusion arises because oblique typefaces are often incorrectly labelled as italics, as is the case with Helvetica Neue 76 Italic.

Helvetica Neue 75 (left) / Helvetica Neue 76 Italic (right)

The italic variation is actually an oblique as it is redrawn to resemble the Roman character.

Client: Barbican Gallery
Design: North
Typographic summary:
Futura Bold Italic, an oblique typeface set, on a nine-degree slanted line

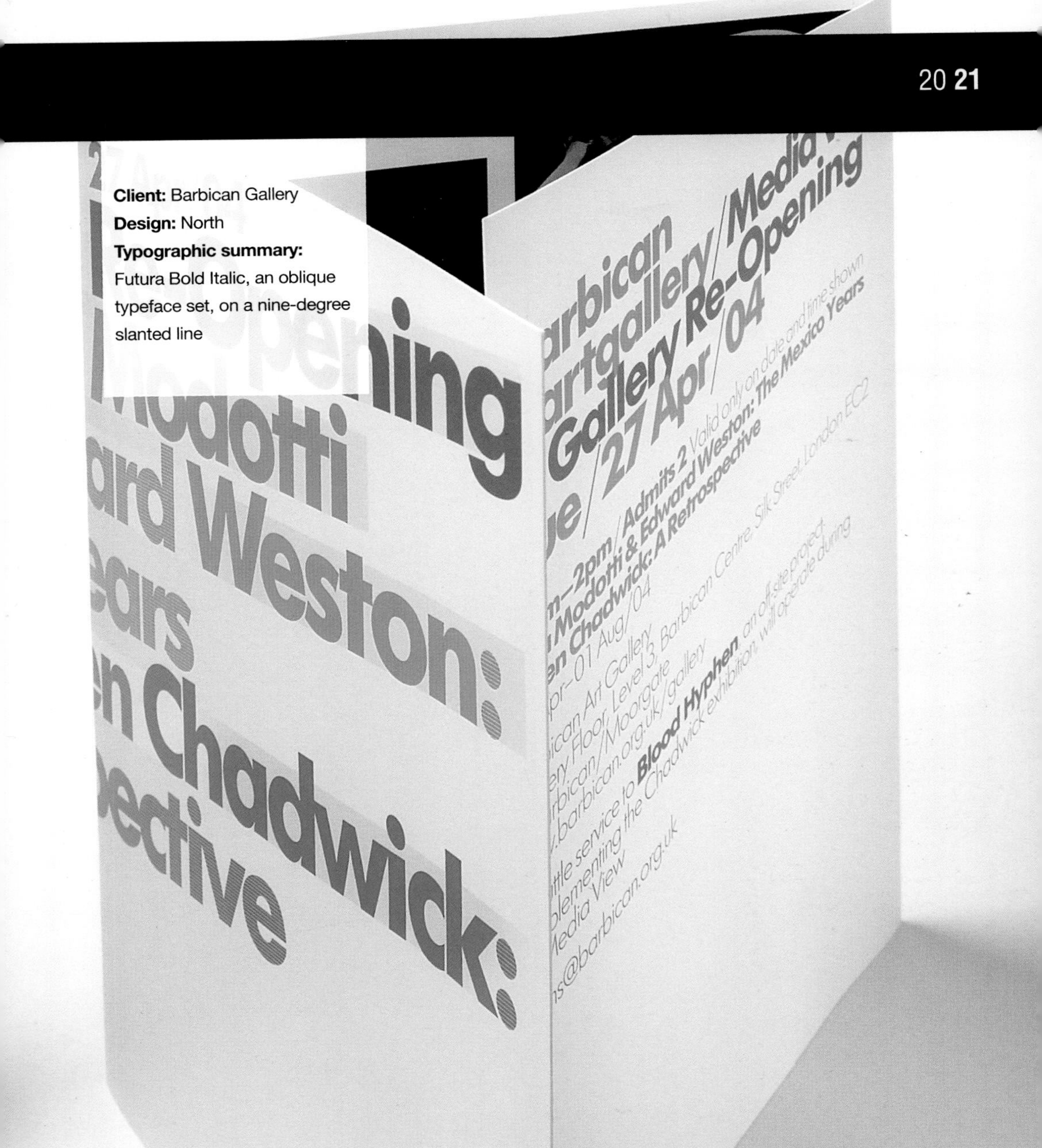

Barbican Gallery Literature

This brochure of forthcoming events was created for the Barbican Centre's Art Gallery by North design studio, and features a version of Futura Bold Italic, which is actually an oblique typeface. In this instance the type is set on a slanted nine-degree line. The consistent use of a single typeface, employed in a single fashion, forms an integral part of the identity, in this instance the typography *is* the identity, as it is the unique setting of the type that becomes memorable and recognisable.

Looking at a typeface

Perhaps one of the most important things to keep in mind when looking at a typeface, or extended typeface family, is that each variation was originally created for a specific function.

The typeface is considered the base component for presenting a message as the examples below from the Minion typeface family demonstrate.

abcdefghijklmnopqrstuvwxyz

Minion Regular

The basic Roman alphabet, used for body text.

ABCDEFGHIJKLMNOPQRSTUVWXYZ

Minion Regular Caps

The standard capitals used for initials and headline text.

ABCDEFGHIJKLMNOPQRSTUVWXYZ

Minion Regular Small Caps

A special set of capitals used for emphasising specific text.

Small caps provide a designer with a subtle means of highlighting a section of text without it standing out too much, or overpowering the surrounding body text. Titles, names and references can thus be distinguished without 'shouting' as they would if they were set in CAPITALS.

A small cap is far more harmonious with the body text because it has been specifically re-cut to have the same width strokes as those of the regular characters. This is not the case with artificial small caps, which have strokes that look thin and give the impression that the characters have been elongated.

Blocks of text are considered easier to read when set in Roman, Old Style or Antiqua, which is to say a combination of majuscule (upper case) and minuscule (lower case) characters. This is because the human eye 'scans' the text using the ascenders and descenders to recognise words rather than constructively reading each and every word. Majuscules share the same height and have fewer visual shortcuts for the eye than minuscules, which have ascending or descending stems that assist scanning.

TEXT SET IN MAJUSCULE CHARACTERS REQUIRES THE READER TO CONSTRUCT THE WORDS BY READING EACH INDIVIDUAL CHARACTER, WHICH CAN BE SLOW AND TIRING.

Lower case letters were developed by Alcuin in the 8th century, these allowed text to be divided into sentences and paragraphs by beginning the first word of a sentence with a capital letter.

Certain languages can look uncomfortable when set in Roman, German for example uses initial capitals at the start of written nouns. This disrupts the scanning motion of the eye: 'I went to the Shop in my Car to buy Food, a Book and a Video'.

S P A C I N G

s p a c i n g

As lower case letters tend to flow into one another it is considered bad typographical practice to letterspace them as this makes the text more difficult to read. Capitals depend less on each other, and so we are therefore more used to viewing and reading them with spacing in place.

Henry Peacock Gallery

Jonathan Ellery, a founding partner of Browns, created this poster for an exhibition at London's Henry Peacock Gallery. In this example, the use of a majuscule text block works well because the design uses a small quantity of large-point letters and a condensed Helvetica bold typeface. This combination means the eye does not have to do much work for the reader to interpret the message. The poster features a quotation from boxer Muhammad Ali, which is foil blocked in to a reflective, metallic paper stock. The poster was produced as a limited edition in four different colour schemes.

Client: Henry Peacock Gallery
Design: Browns
(Jonathan Ellery)
Typographic summary:
Helvetica bold condensed, majuscule text block

Bristol Old Vic

This is an A5, 24-page, four-colour brochure designed by Thirteen for the Bristol Old Vic. The brochure contains details of all the performances to be held at the theatre throughout the first quarter of the 2004 season.

The choice of the Avenir sans-serif typeface set in lower case wonderfully highlights, and visually exploits, the rounded letters in the theatre's name. Interestingly, the designer chose to omit the dot over the letter 'i', perhaps to maintain a clean and uninterrupted x-height line for those letters without ascenders.

The typography forms part of a wider brand identity for Britain's oldest working theatre. This spread, taken from the brochure, shows continued use of the lower case sans-serif typeface for all titles and captions, which enforces the identity design created by Thirteen. However, notice on the inner pages that the dot above the letter 'i' has been restored.

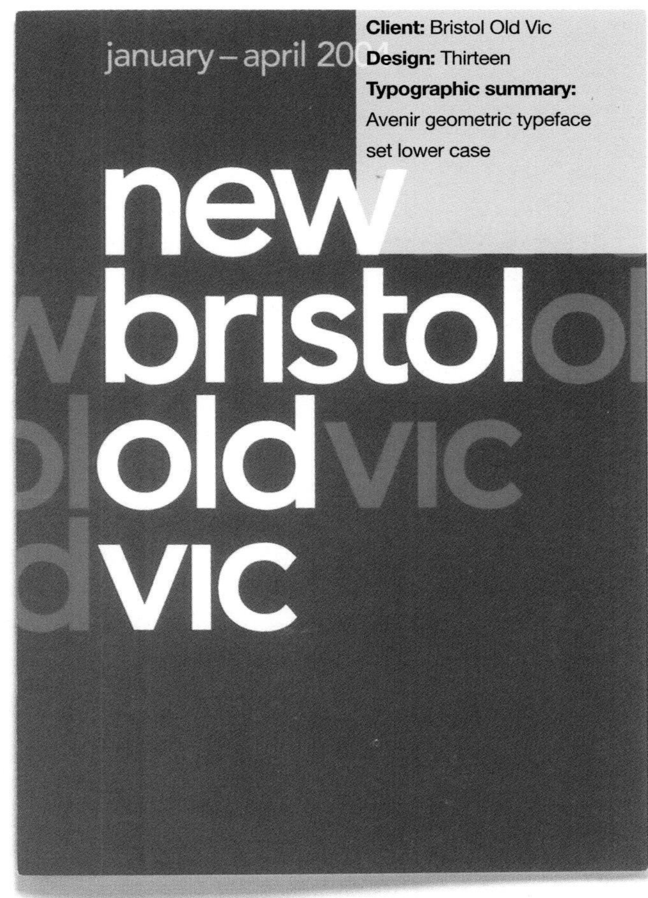

Client: Bristol Old Vic
Design: Thirteen
Typographic summary: Avenir geometric typeface set lower case

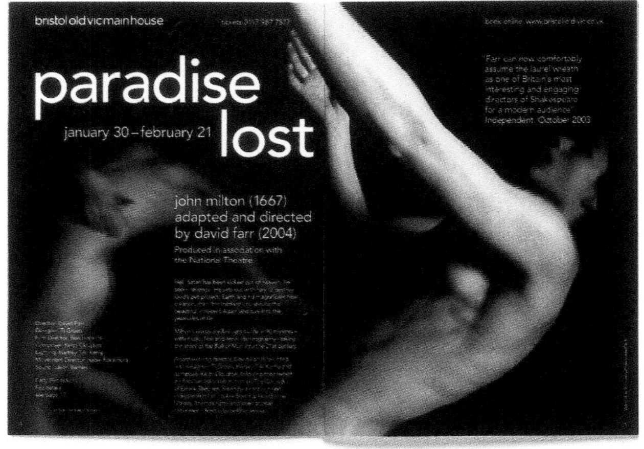

Typeface anatomy

Hoefler Text

Stroke
Refers specifically to the diagonal portion of letterforms such as those in 'N', 'M' or 'Y'. Stems, bars, arms, bowls etc. are collectively referred to as letterform strokes.

Stress
The direction in which a curved stroke changes weight.

Loop
The stroke that encloses, or partially encloses, a counter in a Roman. Sometimes used to describe the cursive 'p' and 'b'.

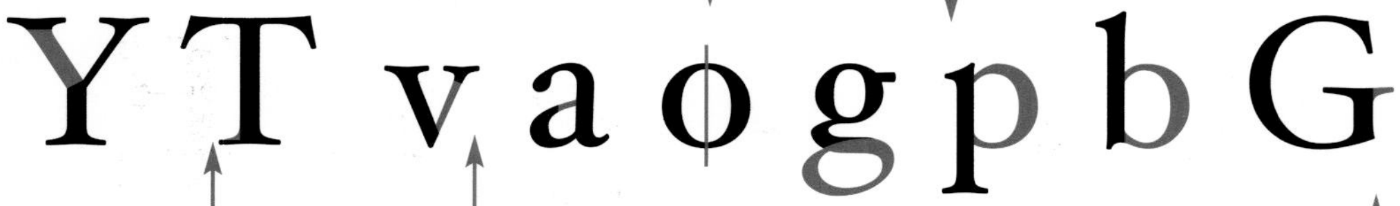

YT vaogpbG

Bracket
The curved portion of a serif that connects it to the stroke.

Hairline
The thinnest stroke in a typeface that has varying widths – can be clearly identified on a 'v' or an 'a'.

Chin
The angled terminal part of the 'G'.

Avenir

Apex
The point formed at the top of a character such as 'A' where the left and right strokes meet.

Shoulder or body
The arch formed on the 'h' or 'n'.

Leg
The lower, downward sloping stroke of the 'K', 'k' and 'R'. Sometimes used for the tail of a 'Q'.

Avhpd KYTF

Vertex
The angle formed at the bottom of a letter where the left and right strokes meet such as with the 'V'.

Ascenders and descenders
An ascender is the part of a letter that extends above the x-height; a descender falls below the baseline.

Terminal
The terminal describes the finish of a stroke. Avenir contains a flat terminal, with no additional decoration. Hoefler Text however, is cut with an acute terminal. Variations include flared, convex, concave and rounded.

Plantin

Tail
The descending stroke on the 'Q', 'K' or 'R'. The descenders on 'g', 'j', 'p', 'q' and 'y' may also be called tails as can the loop of the 'g'.

Link
The part that joins the two bowls of the double-storey 'g'.

Ear
The right side of the bowl of the 'g', the end of an 'r' or 'f' for example.

Serif
The small stroke at the end of a main vertical or horizontal stroke.

Spine
The left-to-right curving stroke in 'S' and 's'.

Arm, bar or crossbar
A horizontal stroke that is open at one or both ends, as seen on the 'T', 'F', 'E' plus the upstroke on the 'K'.

Geo Slab

Stem
The main vertical or diagonal stroke of a letter.

Crotch
Where the leg and arm of the 'K' and 'k' meet.

Crossbar
A horizontal stroke on the 'A' and 'H'. A crossbar joins two stems together.

Cross stroke
The horizontal stroke on the characters 'A', 'H', 'T', 'e', 'f' and 't'. This is sometimes called a crossbar. A cross stroke intersects a single stem.

Bowl / counter
The counter is the empty space inside the body stroke, and is surrounded by the bowl. The counter may be called an eye for the 'e'.

X-height

The 'x-height' is a term applied to the distance between the baseline and the mean line of non-ascending or lower case letters. The letter 'x' is used as a gauge because it is flat at both its top and bottom. The x-height is often used as a layout anchor to produce consistent positioning of images and text blocks.

The x-height is a relative measure specific to the typeface in question. The physical measurement will differ from typeface to typeface even if the point size is the same; as shown in the examples opposite.

As different typefaces of the same point size have different x-heights an optical distortion can occur.

X-height variations between typefaces of the same point size create visual differences. For example, Akzidenz Grotesk (used here), has a comparatively large x-height, this means that less space appears between the lines and there is less room for ascenders and descenders than say, Cochin, which has a smaller x-height. This creates the illusion that there is less leading although it is identical in both examples.

As different typefaces of the same point size have different x-heights an optical distortion can occur.

X-height variations between typefaces of the same point size create visual differences. For example, Akzidenz Grotesk has a comparatively large x-height, this means that less space appears between the lines and there is less room for ascenders and descenders than say, Cochin (used here), which has a smaller x-height. This creates the illusion that there is less leading although it is identical in both examples.

Ascender height
Mean line
Baseline
Descender height

RDLlpx

Cap height
X-height

Cap height and ascender height
Cap height (the height of capital letters), and ascender height (the height of ascenders), are sometimes equal although in certain typefaces they do vary slightly, and the ascender height is marginally higher as demonstrated above.

Eras Demi

Optima

Lucida Sans Roman

Absolute measurements

The white lines below are set 12pts apart and form a grid that has an absolute measurement of 60pts. You will notice that the 60pt type sits within these lines rather than being equal to the measurement.

60 point

The point system

The point measurement system was developed in the 19th century by Pierre Fournier and François Didot. The modern British / American (Anglo-Saxon) point is 1/72 of an inch.

Type point size

The point size of a typeface is measured from the ascent line (top-most ascender), to the descent line (bottom-most descender). The point system was created for metal type. When cast, these blocks or slugs have a space or shoulder to provide some spacing between lines when set. The point size of a font is the measure of the slug and not the letter formed on it.

Relative measurements

Certain typographical measurements are relative – rather than absolute – to the point size of the type being set. An em set in 60pt type is 60pts. An en is equal to half an em. These two measurements are used to set dashes, fractions and spacing, and are useful as the measurement is directly linked to the type; as the type enlarges so does the spacing.

M

M

Ems, Ens and Hyphens

Em

An em is a unit of measurement derived from the width of a square body of the cast upper case 'M'. An em equals the size of a given type, i.e. the em of 60pt type is 60pts. It is used for paragraph indents and denoting nested clauses in North America.

En

An en is a unit of measurement equal to half of one em. It is used in Europe to denote nested clauses. It can also be used to mean 'to' in phrases such as, chapters 10–11, and 1975–1981. An en rule is also used to mean 'and', for example, between two surnames on the spine of a book.

Hyphen

A hyphen is typically one-third the length of an em. It is used to separate parts of compound words, to link the words of a phrase in adjectival hyphenation and to connect the syllables of a word that is split between separate lines.

Client: Diesel

Design: KesselsKramer

Typographic summary:

Pattern created using a wide variety of point sizes

Diesel

A variety of point sizes was used to create this poster for a Diesel campaign, and the resulting pattern of type conveys a sense of natural harmony. The fixed measure and varying point sizes create a dense block of type. This density affords the larger type the appearance of pull-quotes or headlines.

Client: Royal Society of Arts
Design: NB: Studio
Typographic summary:
16-page brochure and broadsheet poster featuring small-point type

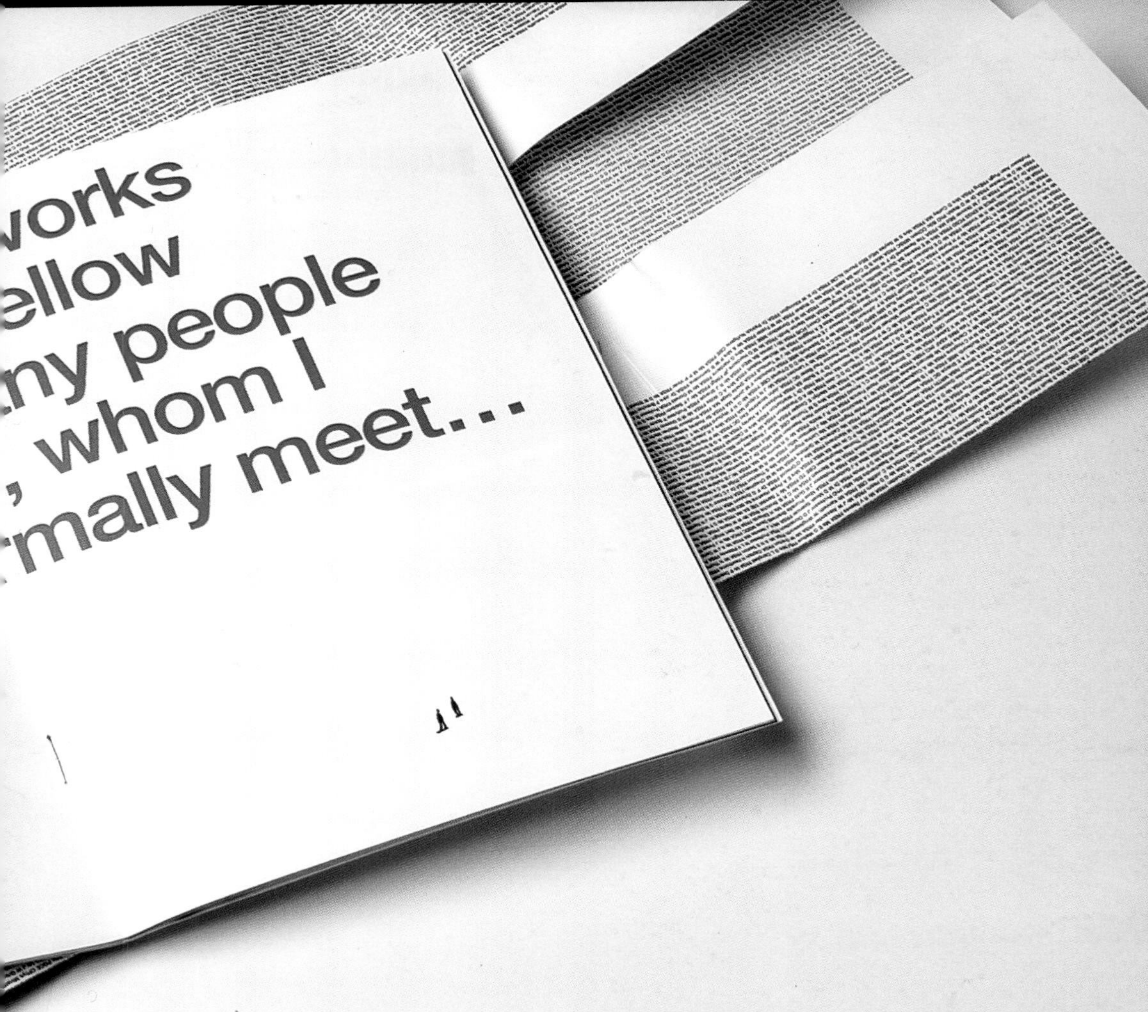

Royal Society of Arts

To do something slightly different for this RSA 16-page brochure – containing a series of illustrations by Tom Gauld – NB: Studio created a broadsheet poster to wraparound and contain the booklet. The poster carries the names of all the fellows of the RSA. There are literally thousands of these to incorporate, which not only indicates the popularity and importance of the organisation but also, on a more practical level, demanded the use of a very small point size in order to print all the information.

A simple hierarchy of 'pattern' and 'text' is created through the variety in point size of the type used. Although all text *can* be read, it's not intended that all text *should* be read, and the dramatic differences in size help to enforce this.

Client: Absolut Label
Design: KesselsKramer
Typographic summary:
Eclectic collection of typefaces used in harmony with their subject matter

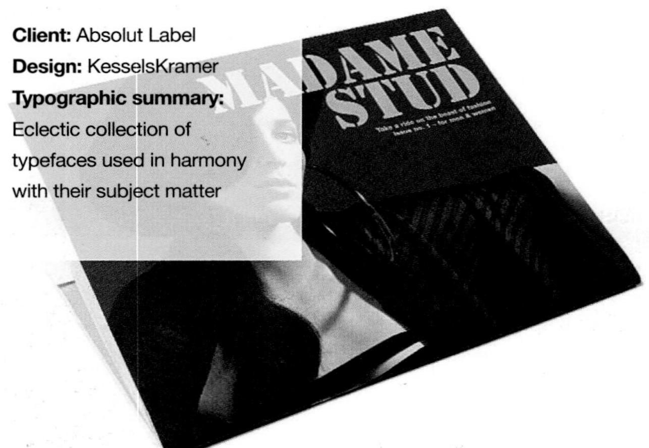

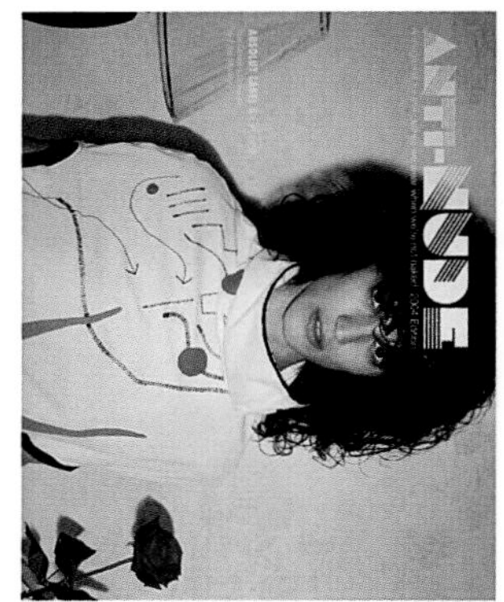

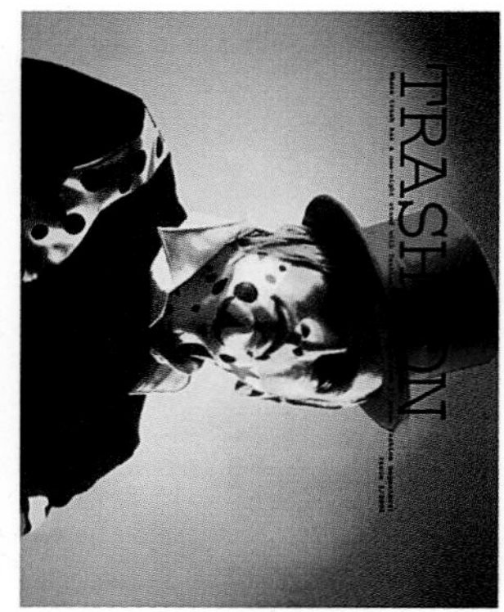

Type Classification

The vast array of typefaces available means that some system of classification is essential, if for no other reason than to simplify the specifications for a piece of work.

Typefaces and type families can be classified according to their inherent characteristics. In order to understand the classification system, and the means by which a typeface is classified, one must be familiar with the terminology used to describe these characteristics. Many typefaces – and much of the terminology used to describe their distinctive features – originate from designs that span the past 500 years, and would have originally been cast in metal or cut in stone. Even now in our digital age, such typefaces still contain the distinct features associated with the physical necessities of the times in which they were created. Typeface classification provides one of those rare occasions when it is appropriate to form a judgement on appearance alone. It is important to obtain an appreciation of how typefaces are classified and the differences between their variations, in order to understand when best to use them within a design.

Typeface classification is based on anatomic characteristics and usually divided between four basic categories: Block, Roman, Gothic and Script (*Human Factors in Engineering Design*, Sanders and McCormick, 1993). Additionally a further category; 'Graphic' (or 'Experimental' or 'Symbol'), accounts for any typefaces that do not naturally fit into any of the four basic categories. The four basic categories can then be further sub-classified: Block (or Blackletter) contains those typefaces based on German manuscript handwriting; Roman houses all the serif typefaces; Gothic contains all the sans-serif typefaces, and finally Script contains those typefaces that mimic handwriting.

Absolut Label (left)

These spreads are taken from the first issue of a fashion magazine sponsored by Absolut. Designed by KesselsKramer, they feature distinctive typefaces for the multiple covers, which reflects the variety of locations featured in the publication.

Clockwise from top left: the cover combines a stencil typeface with clever use of colour to convey a sense of militarism and defiance; 'Greece' uses a retro-futuristic, Graphic typeface; 'Sweden' uses a Geometric typeface with exaggerated descender; 'Russia' demonstrates a Gothic, italic and bold typeface; 'Turkey' uses an extra-light display type with a distinctive dot on the 'i'; 'Brazil' uses a serif typeface; 'Spain' combines hand-drawn type with script and 'France' employs a typewritten typeface, which is used almost as an anti-fashion statement.

Basic classifications

Block, Blackletter, Gothic, Old English, Black or Broken typefaces are based on the ornate writing style prevalent during the Middle Ages. Nowadays, they appear heavy and difficult to read in large text blocks, and seem antiquated.

Blackletter 686

This typeface is based on some of the earliest printing forms, which in turn were based on the script of North European books. Each stroke is accompanied by an offset hairline that produces a light / dark contrast.

Roman

Roman type has proportionally spaced letters and serifs, and was originally derived from Roman inscriptions. It is the most readable type and is commonly used for body text.

Book Antiqua

An old-style typeface, designed by Monotype that is a close copy of Hermann Zapf's Palatino. It has little contrast between stroke weights, which minimises distraction when reading.

Gothic

Gothic, Sans-serif or Lineale typefaces do not have the decorative touches that typify Roman typefaces. Their clean and simple design makes them ideal for display text, but may make them difficult to read in long passages.

Grotesque

Monotype's Grotesque is a 1926 design with simple, clean lines that make it suitable for text use. The absence of serifs is instantly noticeable. The 'g' has a loop rather than being double-storey as seen in serif typefaces.

Script typefaces are designed to imitate handwriting so that when printed the characters appear to be joined up. As with human handwriting, some variations are easier to read than others.

Künstler Script Medium

Künstler Script was designed by Heidelberger Druckmaschinen and has a pronounced slope angle.

Block typefaces

Block, Blackletter, Broken, Old English or Gothic typefaces (not to be confused with sans-serif Gothic), are based on the heavy, ornate writing style that was prevalent during the Middle Ages. Due to the complexity of the letterforms they can be hard to read – particularly if used in large blocks of text – and therefore usually serve a similar function to the decorative use of Scripts or initial capitals. Legibility is however linked to familiarity, thus the Gothic sans-serif styles that are common to us today would be equally hard for Middle Age man to decipher.

ABCDEFGHIJKLMNOPQRSTUVWXYZ
abcdefghijklmnopqrstuvwxyz
1234567890

ABCDEFGHIJKLMNOPQRSTUVWXYZ
abcdefghijklmnopqrstuvwxyz
1234567890

ABCDEFGHIJKLMNOPQRSTUVWXYZ
abcdefghijklmnopqrstuvwxyz
1234567890

Examples of Block typefaces
(Shown left from top to bottom: Engravers Old English, Goudy Text, Fraktur)
These examples demonstrate the ornate and decorative letterforms that contrast hugely with the relatively plain sans-serif typefaces that are in common use today.

This text is set in Cloister Black, which was designed by Morris Fuller Benton and Joseph W Phinney in 1904. As you can see, when a sizeable block of text is set in a Block typeface the ornate letters affect legibility. This has more to do with the text styles that we, as readers, are accustomed to interpreting than being a fault of the typeface. When printing was in its formative years those people that could read would have had little trouble reading this text, but as we are now accustomed to reading simpler and cleaner typefaces the ornate elements of Block confuses the eye and slows down tracking from letter to letter. Legibility can be improved by being more generous with the tracking between letters or the space between words.

Roman typefaces

The decorative serifs of Roman typefaces help the eye track from letter to letter, which is why they are typically used for body text. Roman typefaces comprise the oldest typeface classification and its designs originate from text that was carved into Roman stonework.

Many variations of Roman typefaces have been developed. These variations can be further sub-classified as Old Style Venetian (or Humanist), Old Style Aldine (or Garaldes), Old Style Dutch, Old Style Revival, Transitional, Didone, Slab serif (or Egyptian), Clarendon, and Glyphic.

ABCDEFGHIJKLMNOPQRSTUVWXYZ
abcdefghijklmnopqrstuvwxyz
1234567890

ABCDEFGHIJKLMNOPQRSTUVWXYZ
abcdefghijklmnopqrstuvwxyz
1234567890

ABCDEFGHIJKLMNOPQRSTUVWXYZ
abcdefghijklmnopqrstuvwxyz
1234567890

Examples of Roman typefaces
(Shown left from top to bottom: Cochin, Garamond, Souvenir)
Although these three examples are all classified as serifs they are quite different. In particular take note of the 'Q', 'g', 'J' and 'K'.

Client: Deutsche Bank

Design: Spin

Typographic summary:
Cooper Black combined with hand-drawn imitation, heavily bracketed slur serif (see page 46)

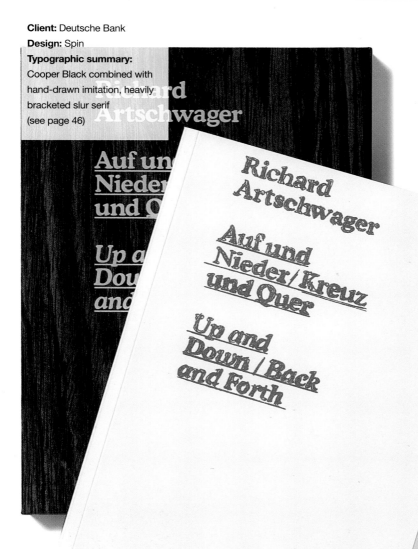

Up and Down / Back and Forth

This catalogue for works by artist Richard Artschwager was created by Spin design studio and features a series of charcoal-on-paper drawings. The inner pages of the book are reflected in the design of the outer. The outer uses Cooper Black – an extra bold old style revival typeface – set in pink against a woodgrain background. Cooper Black is also used for the captions inside the publication. The inner pages feature a reproduction of the cover hand-drawn in charcoal, which is a prelude to the work that follows.

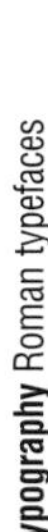

Roman variations

Perhaps it is because the Roman typefaces are such an important mainstay of the printed word that so many variations have been developed. Over time, Roman typefaces have been modified to reflect changes in style, which has resulted in the evolution of new sub-classifications. These sub-classifications help us to more precisely define and distinguish serif typefaces, as the differences between them can be extremely subtle and therefore hard to spot. Some typefaces straddle two or more classification groups to further complicate matters. Remember though the classifications exist to guide and clarify the specifications of a brief.

Old Style

Old style (or Antiqua), typefaces were developed in the 16th and 17th centuries to replace Block typefaces as the standard letterforms in use. They are distinguished by their irregularity and slanted ascender serifs that have low contrast between the thick and thin strokes. They also possess bracketed serifs and a left-inclined stress.

ABCDEFGHIJKLMNOPQRSTUVWXYZ
abcdefghijklmnopqrstuvwxyz 1234567890

Bembo

Bembo was created by Monotype in 1929 for a Stanley Morison project. It is based on a Roman-face cut by Francesco Griffo da Bologna, which Aldus Manutius used to print Pietro Bembo's 1496 publication of *De Aetna*. Morison modified letterforms such as the 'G' to create a typeface with legibility that was suitable for almost any application.

Transitional

Transitional typefaces have a medium contrast between their thick and thin strokes and a lower degree of left-inclined stress. A distinguishing feature of a transitional typeface is a flat or triangular tip where the diagonal strokes meet, as can be seen in the 'W'.

ABCDEFGHIJKLMNOPQRSTUVWXYZ
abcdefghijklmnopqrstuvwxyz 1234567890

Baskerville

Baskerville was designed by John Baskerville in the 18th century. A versatile font, Baskerville is used for both body text and display type. Note the absence of a middle serif on the 'W' and the distinctive capital 'Q'.

Client:
The Cursing Stone Project
Design: Why Not Associates and Gordon Young
Typographic summary: Quotations set in Bembo and sandblasted into rock

The Cursing Stone

The Cursing Stone, created for Glasgow's millennium project, was the result of a collaboration between Why Not Associates and artist Gordon Young. Text quotations from the 1525 *Mother of all Curses* speech by Glaswegian Archbishop Gavin Dunbar were set in Bembo and sandblasted into a 14-tonne boulder.

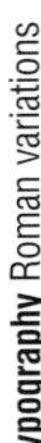

Modern (or Classicist or Empire)

These typefaces were developed towards the end of the 18th century and are recognisable by the high contrast between the thick and thin strokes of each glyph, as well as the flat, unbracketed and often thin serifs.

ABCDEFGHIJKLMNOPQRSTUVWXYZ
abcdefghijklmnopqrstuvwxyz 1234567890

Bodoni

Based on an 18th-century design by Gianbattista Bodoni this typeface has hairline serifs and heavy down strokes.

Slab Serif (or Egyptian)

Slab-serif typefaces are distinguished by larger, square serifs, which were considered to be bolder than those of their predecessors. Slab-serif typefaces can be further classified into Clarendon and typewriter styles.

ABCDEFGHIJKLMNOPQRSTUVWXYZ
abcdefghijklmnopqrstuvwxyz 1234567890

Serifa

Serifa has a solid appearance and simple slab serifs that do not dominate the characters.

Clarendon

A slab serif sub-classification, which uses subtle serif brackets.

ABCDEFGHIJKLMNOPQRSTUVWXYZ
abcdefghijklmnopqrstuvwxyz 1234567890

Century Schoolbook

Has a greater contrast between the thick and thin strokes than those of slab serif typefaces, this is particularly noticeable on the serifs. The tail of the 'Q' penetrates the counter and the 'J' has a prominent tail dot.

Typewriter

A sub-classification of slab-serif typefaces, these have serifs of equal width to the stem of the character.

ABCDEFGHIJKLMNOPQRSTUVWXYZ
abcdefghijklmnopqrstuvwxyz 1234567890

American Typewriter

This typeface has additional finials, reminiscent of ink-traps that appear in non-digitised typewriter typefaces.

Client: Fundacío Gala-Salvador Dalí
Design: bis
Typographic summary: Bodoni typography and inventive use of brace

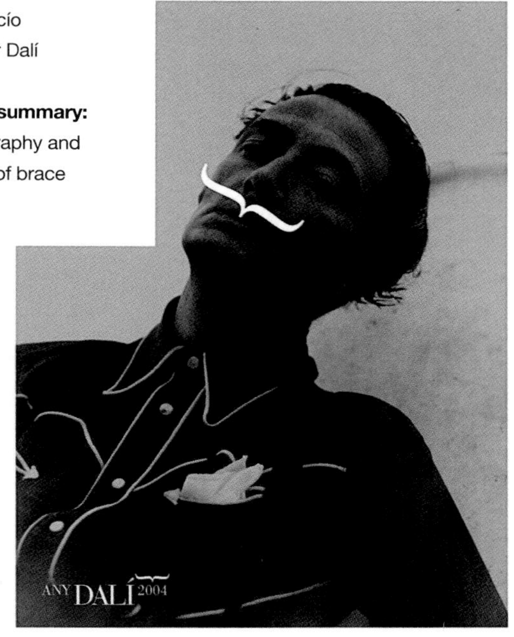

Dalí 2004

Spanish design studio bis was asked to develop an identity to mark the celebrations of the 100th anniversary of the birth of artist Salvador Dalí. Photographs of the surrealist painter were used as the central iconic image in the various pieces of work with typography in Bodoni; Dalí's favourite typeface. A brace (or curly bracket), was inserted over Dalí's face in each photograph as a clever imitation of his famous moustache.

Serif variations

There are many ornate and noticeable serif styles available and most are grouped within the following categories. As serifs, particularly the more ornate ones, are frequently used for display type, it is important to consider them carefully.

SLUR SERIF

Cooper Black – designed by Oswald B. Cooper in 1921, this typeface was ahead of its time.

Slur serifs are rounded, almost 'inflated' variations; although ill-defined, these serifs are highly distinctive.

BRACKETED SERIF

Berkeley – based on California and originally designed for the University Press by Frederic Goudy.

Common in many typefaces, bracketed serifs have a curve that creates a smooth transition from serif to stroke.

UNBRACKETED SERIF

Memphis – Geometric typeface designed by Rudolf Wolf.

Unbracketed serif typefaces have equal, or monoline, serif and stroke widths.

BRACKETED SLAB SERIF

Clarendon – confusingly both a typeface (see page 44) and a font.

Bracketed slab serifs have monoline serifs 'softened' by joining blends.

UNBRACKETED SLAB SERIF

Egiziano Classic Antique Black – designed by Dennis Ortiz-Lopez.

Unbracketed slab serifs carry the heaviest serifs with no joining blends.

WEDGE SERIF

Meridien – Adrian Frutiger's font, specifically designed to contain no straight strokes.

Wedge serifs display a triangular serif shape.

HAIRLINE SERIF

Bodoni – Morris Fuller Benton's cutting of Gianbattista Bodoni's masterpiece typeface.

Hairline serifs have disproportionally thin serifs, but often retain decorative tails, terminals and ears.

Peter Blake Invitation

The typography on this exhibition invitation is developed from found objects belonging to Peter Blake – some of which appeared on his album sleeve design for the Paul Weller's 'Stanley Road'. As the title suggests, the exhibition is about the commer art practice of Blake. The pronounced wedge- d serifs make a distinctive design statemen

Client: London Institute Gallery
Design: Webb & Webb
Typographic summary: Found typographical objects used instead of traditional characters. Typeface with distinctive wedge serif

Gothic typefaces

Gothic typefaces – also called sans-serif typefaces – have been in existence for more than 100 years. The absence of any serifs, whilst providing a clean letterform, can impinge on the legibility of the body text. Historically typographers have tried to address this issue by cutting Gothic typefaces suitable for setting body text. Even so Gothic typefaces remain limited in their use and are more commonly used in short bursts as headings or other display functions. Gothic typefaces always have a 'g' with a tail rather than the double-storey 'g' used in some serif typefaces.

ABCDEFGHIJKLMNOPQRSTUVWXYZ
abcdefghijklmnopqrstuvwxyz
1234567890

ABCDEFGHIJKLMNOPQRSTUVWXYZ
abcdefghijklmnopqrstuvwxyz
1234567890

ABCDEFGHIJKLMNOPQRSTUVWXYZ
abcdefghijklmnopqrstuvwxyz
1234567890

Examples of Gothic typefaces
(Shown left from top to bottom: Din, Folio, Frutiger)
These examples illustrate the variety of stroke weights and openness that sans-serif typefaces possess. Folio and Frutiger are bolder in appearance and have rounder letterforms. By comparison, Din is lighter and more condensed.

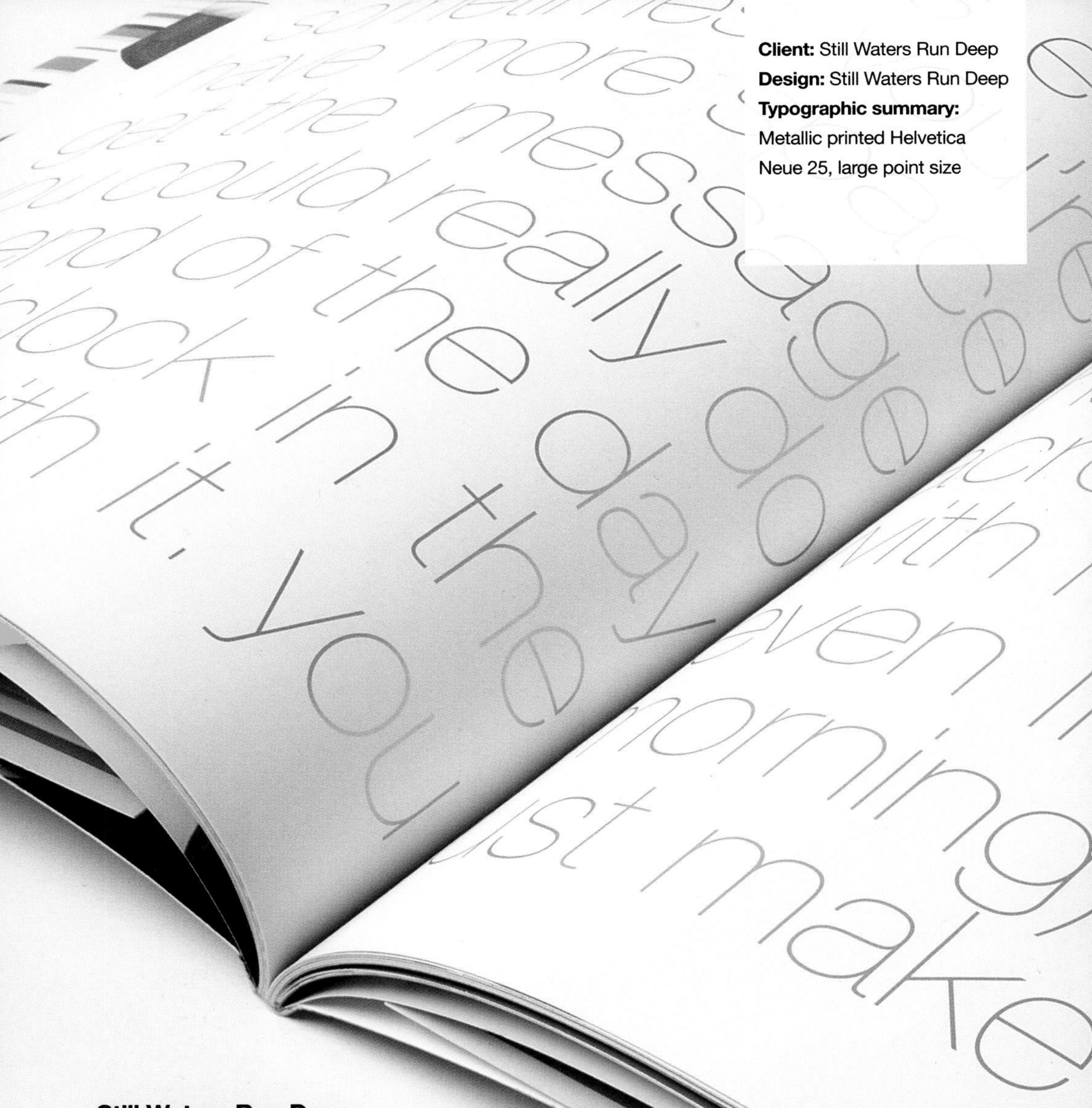

Client: Still Waters Run Deep
Design: Still Waters Run Deep
Typographic summary:
Metallic printed Helvetica Neue 25, large point size

Still Waters Run Deep

This brochure was produced for the tenth birthday of design studio Still Waters Run Deep. The use of Helvetica Neue 25, demonstrates the simple beauty of lower case typographic detailing such as the terminal tail stroke on the 'a'. This typography is deceptively simple. As the letters used are set in a large point size, the tracking and the kerning (see pages 94–99), are far more important than when text is typeset in a smaller point size (body text for example). Belonging to an extended type family (see page 62), Helvetica Neue 25 is the thinnest version of the typeface and when combined with the metallic ink printing, it creates an elegant typographical statement.

Gothic variations

Gothic, or sans-serif, typefaces were developed later than their Roman counterparts, and within the Gothic classification typographers have created an imaginative and widely different body of typefaces. Consequently, a variety of sub-categories have evolved to more precisely define them.

Distinctions between different Gothic typefaces can be readily and easily seen in a study of the letters 'a', 'e', 'g', 'G', 'M', 'R' and 'y' as the examples below demonstrate.

Grotesque

Grotesque typefaces have a more condensed form than those of Neo Grotesques and possess a 'g' with a double-storey (rather than a loop), and a 'G' with a chin.

ABCDEFGHIJKLMNOPQRSTUVWXYZ

abcdefghijklmnopqrstuvwxyz 1234567890

Alternate Gothic No. 2

Alternative Gothic No. 2 has a condensed character body.

Neo Grotesque

Neo-Grotesque typefaces have broader characters than those of Grotesques and possess a 'g' with a loop (rather than a double-storey), and a 'G' with a chin.

ABCDEFGHIJKLMNOPQRSTUVWXYZ

abcdefghijklmnopqrstuvwxyz 1234567890

Akzidenz Grotesk BQ

Akzidenz Grotesk BQ has rounded strokes and a full shape.

The Moving Picture Company (right)

This design, created by Form Design for The Moving Picture Company, uses a white foil (see page 146) on a high-gloss white board. This adds a tactile element to the design and also produces a subtle white-on-white effect, as the letters appear when the viewing angle and the reflected light are changed. The text in this example is set in Akzidenz Grotesk and clearly displays the main characteristics of the Neo-Grotesque typefaces.

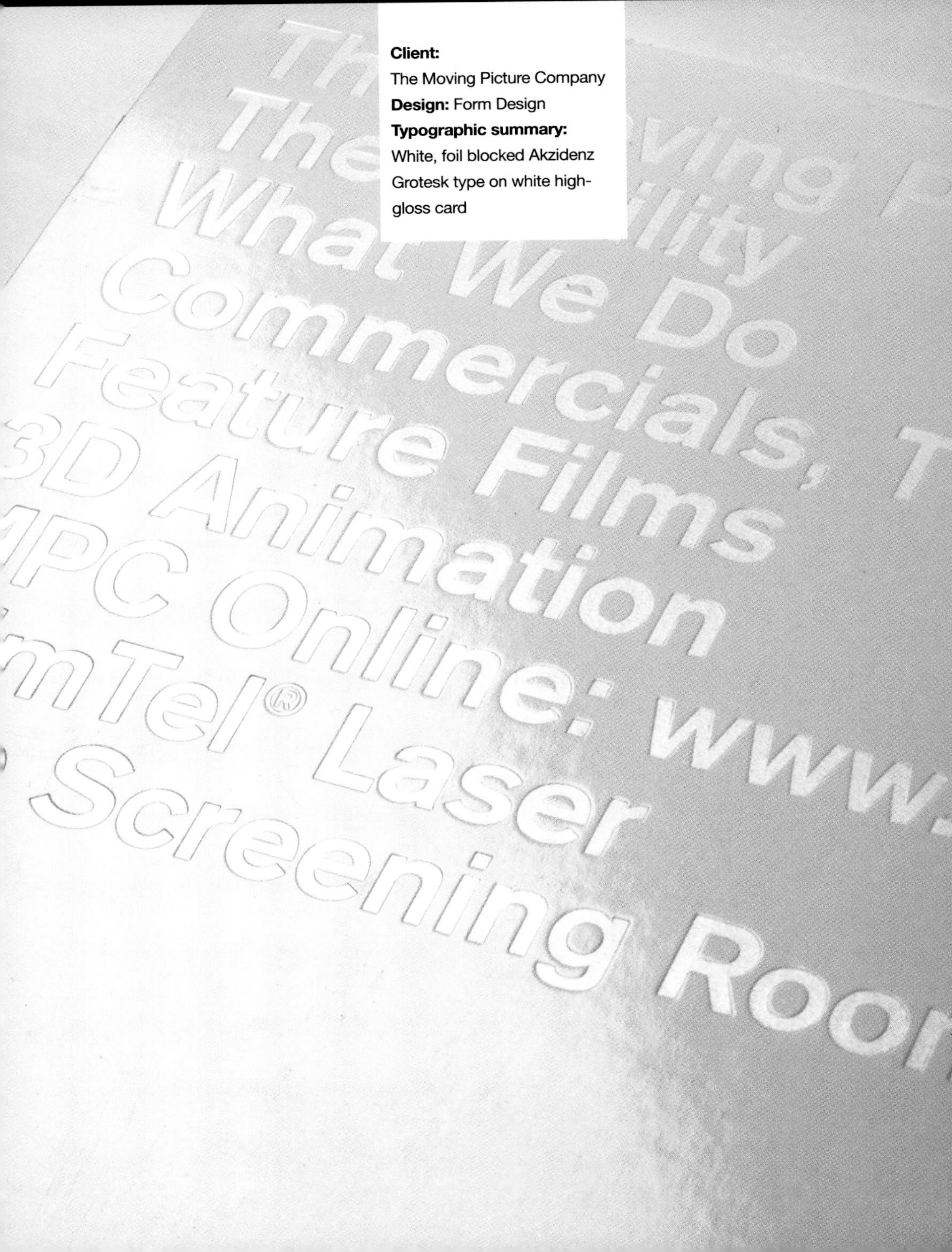

Client:
The Moving Picture Company
Design: Form Design
Typographic summary:
White, foil blocked Akzidenz Grotesk type on white high-gloss card

Geometric

Geometric is a descriptive term applied to certain Gothic typefaces and also to some Graphic typefaces (see page 58). The Geometric Gothic variations have a very rounded shape and are distinguishable by their splayed 'M', 'N', 'V' and 'W' characters. The leg of the 'R' joins the bowl near the stem and the 'G' is chinless.

ABCDEFGHIJKLMNOPQRSTUVWXYZ
abcdefghijklmnopqrstuvwxyz 1234567890

Futura BQ

Futura BQ demonstrates the splayed 'M', 'N', 'V' and 'W', the leg of the 'R' joining the loop near the stem and the chinless 'G'.

Humanistic

Humanistic typefaces are similar to Geometric ones as they also possess splayed 'M', 'N', 'V' and 'W', a chinless 'G' and an 'R' with a leg joining the bowl near the stem. However, they have more stroke weight contrast and a double-storey 'g'.

ABCDEFGHIJKLMNOPQRSTUVWXYZ
abcdefghijklmnopqrstuvwxyz 1234567890

Optima

Optima has the double-storey 'g' and shows the contrast between the weights of higher strokes.

Square

Square typefaces, as the name suggests, have squared characters rather than rounded characters. The 'g' has a tail and the 'Q' has a tail that crosses the bowl. The 'G' is chinless.

ABCDEFGHIJKLMNOPQRSTUVWXYZ
abcdefghijklmnopqrstuvwxyz 1234567890

Eurostile

Eurostile clearly has a squarer appearance when compared to the other typefaces shown on this spread.

Yauatcha (right)

This stationery for Yauatcha, by North design studio, uses Futura SB Extra Light, tightly tracked to give a very elegant and controlled appearance. The stationery uses a bold, abstracted pattern of tea plant growth on the reverse that shows through the page. The fluorescent circular pattern on the reverse invokes the impression of liquid, and contrasts with the serene nature of the typography.

Client: Yauatcha
Design: North
Typographic summary:
Tightly tracked Futura SB Extra Light

15 BROADWICK STREET
LONDON W1F 0DL
TEL 020 7494 8888
FAX 020 7494 8889
EMAIL MAIL@YAUATCHA.COM
WITH COMPLIMENTS

丘記茶苑 YAUATCHA

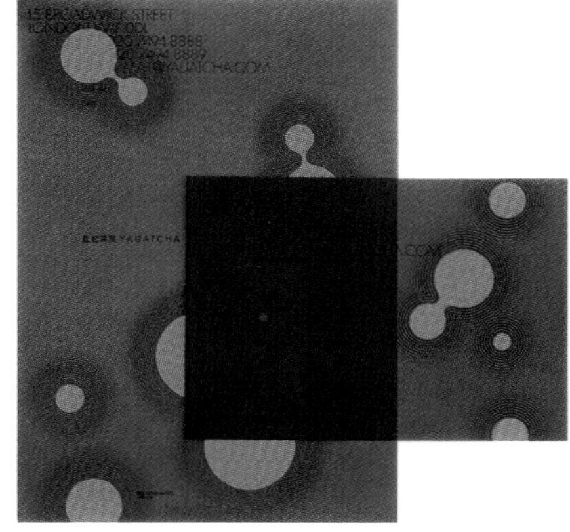

Rounded variations possess rounded – rather than squared-off – stroke endings, which results in slightly more relaxed and visually appealing letterforms. Many of these rounded variations find their origin in other typefaces (for example, Helvetica Rounded is based on standard Helvetica). The rounding of these established typefaces creates an open and spacious appearance.

ABCDEFGHIJKLMNOPQRSTUVWXYZ
abcdefghijklmnopqrstuvwxyz 1234567890
ABCDEFGHIJKLMNOPQRSTUVWXYZ
abcdefghijklmnopqrstuvwxyz 1234567890

Helvetica Rounded

A rounded version of Max Miedinger's classic design; Haas Grotesk. Later named Helvetica (an adaptation of the the Latin name for Switzerland ('Helvetier'). The rounded variation is a direct adaptation of the original sans-serif.

ABCDEFGHIJKLMNOPQRSTUVWXYZ
abcdefghijklmnopqrstuvwxyz 1234567890

Vag Rounded Black

Designed by Adrian Williams for Volkswagen in 1979, VAG Rounded exhibits similar characteristics to Helvetica Rounded but there are noticeable differences. The letter 'a' is noticeably geometric and the lower case 'j' and 'y' are rendered without the curved stroke at the end. The vertical stems of the upper case 'M' are oblique.

ABCDEFGHIJKLMNOPQRSTUVWXYZ
abcdefghijklmnopqrstuvwxyz 1234567890

Arial Rounded Extra Bold

A rounded version of Arial – with curved stroke ends like Helvetica Rounded, but with a chinless 'G' as found in Vag Rounded.

Bringing Architecture Home (right)

This concise guide for homeowners about the advantages of hiring an architect was a free cover mount designed for *Elle Decoration* magazine. Vag Rounded was selected as the typeface because its soft edges are friendly and homely, and reflect the nature of the brochure. This also makes hiring an architect seem less intimidating.

Client: RIBA, Arts Council for England, Habitat
Design: Gavin Ambrose
Typographic summary: Vag Rounded lower case used to project friendliness and homeliness

bringing
architecture
home

what an architect can do for you...

Script typefaces

Script typefaces were created to mimic handwriting and indeed some, such as Pushkin, were based on the handwriting of a specific person. Many have extended termination strokes so that they link together, much like the handwriting they are intended to resemble. They are neither classified as Roman or Gothic, as they may share attributes of each.

As Script typefaces are difficult to read in large text blocks, their usage is usually confined to providing supplementary decorative details such as brand names or captions.

ABCDEFGHIJKLMNOPQRSTUVWXYZ
abcdefghijklmnopqrstuvwxyz
1234567890

ABCDEFGHIJKLMNOPQRSTUVWXYZ
abcdefghijklmnopqrstuvwxyz
1234567890

ABCDEFGHIJKLMNOPQRSTUVWXYZ
abcdefghijklmnopqrstuvwxyz
1234567890

Examples of Script typefaces
(Shown left from top to bottom: Flemish Script, Berthold Script, Zapf Chancery)
Script typefaces vary in legibility depending upon how elaborate they are. Flemish Script is considerably more difficult to decipher than Zapf Chancery due to its ornate strokes.

Kew

For the corporate identity for Kew, SEA Design chose to interpret the brand name in a script. The typeface is soft, feminine, personal and friendly, and on the bags shown is complemented by atmospheric background photography by Richard Learoyd.

Client: Kew
Design: SEA Design
Typographic summary: Hand-drawn script, which creates a feminine and personal feel

Graphic typefaces

Graphic typefaces contain characters that could be considered images in their own right. These experimental variations include the widest array of styles with varying degrees of legibility. Often they may be designed for specific, themed purposes. Characters may absorb the attributes of whatever they are being used to communicate, or they may provide an image connection to the subject matter.

Graphic typefaces can emphasise the drama of a design, although their complexity can adversely affect legibility and so are unsuitable for use in body text.

abcdefghijklmnopqrstuvwxyz
1234567890

ABCDEFGHIJKLMNOPQRSTUVWXYZ
1234567890

abcdefghijklmnopqrstuvwxyz

Graphic typeface examples
(Shown left from top to bottom: Pop Led, Dynomoe, Dr No)
These decorative typefaces are most effective in display texts such as headlines or brand names. The eye has to work too hard for information when typefaces such as Pop Led and Dr No are used extensively.

Client: Caro Communications
Design: Form Design
Typographic summary:
Bespoke letters formed from a single round-cornered square

Caro Communications

This identity, created for public relations firm Caro Communications, features a logotype whose letters are formed by the rounded corners of a square. In this experimental typeface, characters are only legible through their shared relationships – the 'c' and the 'o' provide enough 'code' to decipher the other letters. These very graphic characters, can become unreadable in isolation so their use is restricted to the main marque, with a secondary sans-serif typeface used for additional information.

Client: Shakespeare's Globe
Design: Pentagram (Angus Hyland with Charlie Hanson)
Typographic summary: Combination of historical and contemporary typefaces

Antony and Cleopatra
by William Shakespeare

1999

Setting Type

Setting type sounds straightforward enough – you put it down on the page and manipulate it – but the skill lays in knowing how to manipulate it in order to produce the results you require. To this end, there are various techniques and structures to help a designer control and set type effectively on the page. An understanding of these basics allows the designer to produce a coherent and effective design by controlling and harmonising the various typographical elements that it contains. In some instances, as in the example opposite, type elements are selected for their historical evocations, as well as their contemporary aesthetics.

The effective use of type is a combination of understanding typefaces – which was covered in the previous section – and controlling their usage so that they express the ideas that you want them to. When this combination is applied, typography that is thoughtfully and precisely set, will enhance the meaning of a given text.

As previously discussed, even the relatively simple task of selecting a typeface requires informed decision making. Graphic communication is very much a sum of its parts – typeface selection, as we've seen, can have a dramatic impact on a design, but equally the finer nuances of typesetting can alter the way we perceive and interpret messages.

Thoughtful setting of type enables the controlled imparting of information. Whether you intended the work to be immediate, stylistic, historic, anarchic or modern; the basics of setting type can help you achieve it.

Shakespeare's Globe

Play was published in 2003 to document and celebrate the first five seasons at the rebuilt Shakespeare's Globe Theatre in London. Designed by Angus Hyland with Charlie Hanson at Pentagram, the book conveys the sense of history associated with Shakespeare's Globe. Minion was the typeface used for the front cover, heading and introductory paragraphs, specifically selected to recall the typography used by printers during the days of the original Globe Theatre. This historic link is reinforced by the coarse, natural stock used for the cover.

The rebuilt Shakespeare's Globe is a modern theatre, and this fact is reflected in the use of Helvetica Neue for the body text. It gives a contemporary tone that underlines the relevance of the theatre (and Shakespeare) to contemporary audiences.

Type families

A type family incorporates all the variations of a particular typeface, including the range of different weights, widths and italics. They are a useful design tool because they provide the designer with options that work together in a consistent way.

Shown below as an example of an extended type family are some of the many versions of Gill Sans. The variety offered by such a comprehensive typeface family is suitable for everything from footnotes to posters, body text to headlines, without the need for any additional typefaces.

ABCDEFGHIJKLMNOPQRSTUVWXYZ abcdefghijklmnopqrstuvwxyz 1234567890
ABCDEFGHIJKLMNOPQRSTUVWXYZ ABCDEFGHIJKLMNOPQRSTUVWXYZ 1234567890
ABCDEFGHIJKLMNOPQRSTUVWXYZ abcdefghijklmnopqrstuvwxyz 1234567890
ABCDEFGHIJKLMNOPQRSTUVWXYZ abcdefghijklmnopqrstuvwxyz 1234567890
ABCDEFGHIJKLMNOPQRSTUVWXYZ abcdefghijklmnopqrstuvwxyz 1234567890
ABCDEFGHIJKLMNOPQRSTUVWXYZ abcdefghijklmnopqrstuvwxyz 1234567890
ABCDEFGHIJKLMNOPQRSTUVWXYZ abcdefghijklmnopqrstuvwxyz 1234567890
ABCDEFGHIJKLMNOPQRSTUVWXYZ ABCDEFGHIJKLMNOPQRSTUVWXYZ 1234567890
ABCDEFGHIJKLMNOPQRSTUVWXYZ abcdefghijklmnopqrstuvwxyz 1234567890
ABCDEFGHIJKLMNOPQRSTUVWXYZ abcdefghijklmnopqrstuvwxyz 1234567890
ABCDEFGHIJKLMNOPQRSTUVWXYZ abcdefghijklmnopqrstuvwxyz 1234567890
ABCDEFGHIJKLMNOPQRSTUVWXYZ abcdefghijklmnopqrstuvwxyz 1234567890
ABCDEFGHIJKLMNOPQRSTUVWXYZ ABCDEFGHIJKLMNOPQRSTUVWXYZ 1234567890
ABCDEFGHIJKLMNOPQRSTUVWXYZ abcdefghijklmnopqrstuvwxyz 1234567890
ABCDEFGHIJKLMNOPQRSTUVWXYZ abcdefghijklmnopqrstuvwxyz 1234567890
ABCDEFGHIJKLMNOPQRSTUVWXYZ abcdefghijklmnopqrstuvwxyz 1234567890
ABCDEFGHIJKLMNOPQRSTUVWXYZ ABCDEFGHIJKLMNOPQRSTUVWXYZ 1234567890
ABCDEFGHIJKLMNOPQRSTUVWXYZ abcdefghijklmnopqrstuvwxyz 1234567890
ABCDEFGHIJKLMNOPQRSTUVWXYZ abcdefghijklmnopqrstuvwxyz 1234567890
ABCDEFGHIJKLMNOPQRSTUVWXYZ abcdefghijklmnopqrstuvwxyz 1234567890
ABCDEFGHIJKLMNOPQRSTUVWXYZ abcdefghijklmnopqrstuvwxyz 1234567890

Gill Sans

The above typefaces are variations from the Gill Sans sans-serif family, designed by Eric Gill in the 1920s, and based on the typeface used by London Underground. In addition to the many weights and styles, numerals are presented in very different ways for this ever popular typeface. The naming system applied here can appear confusing; it begins with Gill Sans Light, then Gill Sans Light Small Caps, Gill Sans Light Italic and Gill Sans Light Italic Old Style Figures, and continues through the different book weights, the bolds, the blacks, the heavies and the ultras, all with their own small capital and italic variations.

One solution to the confusion of naming type families can be seen clearly if you arrange the weights on a grid, rather than in a column. Here there are four typeface styles: a sans-serif, a semi-sans, a semi-serif and a serif. The sans-serif and the semi-sans, which are more useful in body text, carry a wide range of weights. The 'quirkier' semi-serif and serif, which are more suited to display purposes, carry a reduced range of weights.

Sans-Serif	Semi-Sans	Semi-Serif	Serif
Rotis Sans-Serif Light	Rotis Semi-Sans Light		
Rotis Sans-Serif Light Italic	*Rotis Semi-Sans Light Italic*		
Rotis Sans-Serif Regular	Rotis Semi-Sans Regular	Rotis Semi-Serif Regular	Rotis Serif Regular
Rotis Sans-Serif Italic	*Rotis Semi-Sans Italic*		*Rotis Serif Italic*
Rotis Sans-Serif Bold	Rotis Semi-Sans Bold	Rotis Semi-Serif Bold	Rotis Serif Bold
Rotis Sans-Serif Extra Bold	**Rotis Semi-Sans Extra Bold**		

Rotis

Cut in 1989, Rotis is a typeface family that incorporates both serif and sans-serif styles in various combinations. It also includes a range of weights or 'colours' such as light, regular, bold and black. Rotis exhibits a current trend for designing typefaces that are available in both serif and sans-serif varieties, and even mixtures of both. These combinations can offer flexibility, and semi-sans in particular offers a typeface that is easy to read (like a serif), but with the more rigid nature of a sans-serif.

Stone Sans	Stone Serif	Stone Informal
STONE SANS REGULAR	STONE SERIF REGULAR	STONE INFORMAL REGULAR
STONE SANS ITALIC	*STONE SERIF ITALIC*	*STONE INFORMAL ITALIC*
STONE SANS SEMI-BOLD	STONE SERIF SEMI-BOLD	STONE INFORMAL SEMI-BOLD
STONE SANS SEMI-BOLD ITALIC	*STONE SERIF SEMI-BOLD ITALIC*	*STONE INFORMAL SEMI-BOLD ITALIC*
STONE SANS BOLD	**STONE SERIF BOLD**	**STONE INFORMAL BOLD**
STONE SANS BOLD ITALIC	***STONE SERIF BOLD ITALIC***	***STONE INFORMAL BOLD ITALIC***

Stone

Stone is an extended typeface family designed by Sumner Stone that contains serif, sans-serif, and informal styles that all have a Roman and italic version in three weights: medium, semi-bold, and bold. The informal typeface contains a mixture of sans-serif and serif characteristics.

Adrian Frutiger is prominent in the pantheon of typographers due to the classification grid he developed to show the relationships between the different weights and widths of his Univers typeface.

		53	63	73	83
		54	*64*	*74*	*84*
	45	55	65	75	85
	46	*56*	*66*	*76*	*86*
	47	57	67		
	48	*58*	*68*		
39	49	59			

Univers

Adrian Frutiger created the Univers typeface family in 1951. A key reason for its success was the numbering system Frutiger developed to show the width and weight relationships between the original 21 cuts. This numbering system is known as Frutiger's grid. The first number in each pairing relates to the weight – three is the narrowest and eight the heaviest. The second number in each pairing relates to width – three is the most extended and nine the most condensed. Additionally, odd numbers indicate Roman and even numbers designate italics.

Glypha 45 | Glypha 57 | **Glypha 75**

Glypha

Adrian Frutiger designed Glypha, a serif typeface in 1977. This type family follows the same numbering system he developed with Univers.

Frutiger 45 | Frutiger 45 | **Frutiger 45**

Frutiger

Adrian Frutiger designed Frutiger in 1975 for what is now Charles de Gaulle International Airport in Paris. It is a general purpose Humanist sans-serif that again follows the numbering system he developed with Univers.

Helvetica Neue 25 | **Helvetica Neue 53** | Helvetica Neue 39

Helvetica Neue

Helvetica Neue was designed by Max Miedinger, and others at the Haas'sche Schriftgiesserei, by modifying Helvetica letterforms for the Linotype system. In 1983 David Stempel redesigned and digitised it to create a self-contained typeface family, which now has 51 different typeface weights.

To achieve clarity and a uniform feel many designers restrict themselves to using only two typeface weights from a particular family, as this is enough to establish a typographic hierarchy without unnecessary elaboration.

Typographical hierarchy

This is usually established using two weights of one typeface. Here the header is set in Helvetica Bold 75 and the body text in Helvetica Roman 55. The difference between the two weights is sufficient for it to be clearly distinguished without the two weights appearing unrelated.

Typographical harmony

This is unattainable if the difference between the two weights is too extreme. Here the solid black appearance of Helvetica Black 95 in the header swallows up the fineness of the Helvetica Ultra Light 25 used in the body text.

Typographical difference

This will pass unnoticed if you use typefaces that are next to each other on the grid. Here the header is set in Helvetica Bold 85 and is accompanied by body text set in Helvetica Bold 75, but the difference between them is barely noticeable.

Using multiple typefaces

Although it is possible to complete a design using a single typeface, it is common for more than one to be used. The use of two or more typefaces immediately presents the opportunity to create a hierarchy, which can greatly ease navigation around a publication.

There are no hard and fast rules concerning which typefaces, or indeed how many, to choose for a design. Certain jobs may require more typographical variety and extreme differences in the type styles used while in others, the simple addition of a secondary typeface may be used to differentiate footnotes or marginalia from the body text. Below are some general considerations that may prove helpful.

Distinctive typefaces are often used for titles[†]
The body text can then be selected to be used in conjunction with this. Frequently one will be a Roman typeface and the other a Gothic[††].

Selected typefaces need to have flexibility[1]

† *Souvenir*
†† *Helvetica Roman 55*
1 *Often a different version of the body text typeface will be used for footnotes and marginalia. In this case Helvetica Italic 56.*

Of course this can be reversed,[†]
as long as there is a difference between the titling typeface and the body text[††].

† *Impact*
†† *Bembo*

If the typefaces are too similar though,[†]
the differences between one typeface and another[††] may go unnoticed.

† *Swiss*
†† *Akzidenz Grotesk*

Client: Haunch of Venison
Design: Spin
Typographic summary:
Reversal of typeface hierarchy to add variation

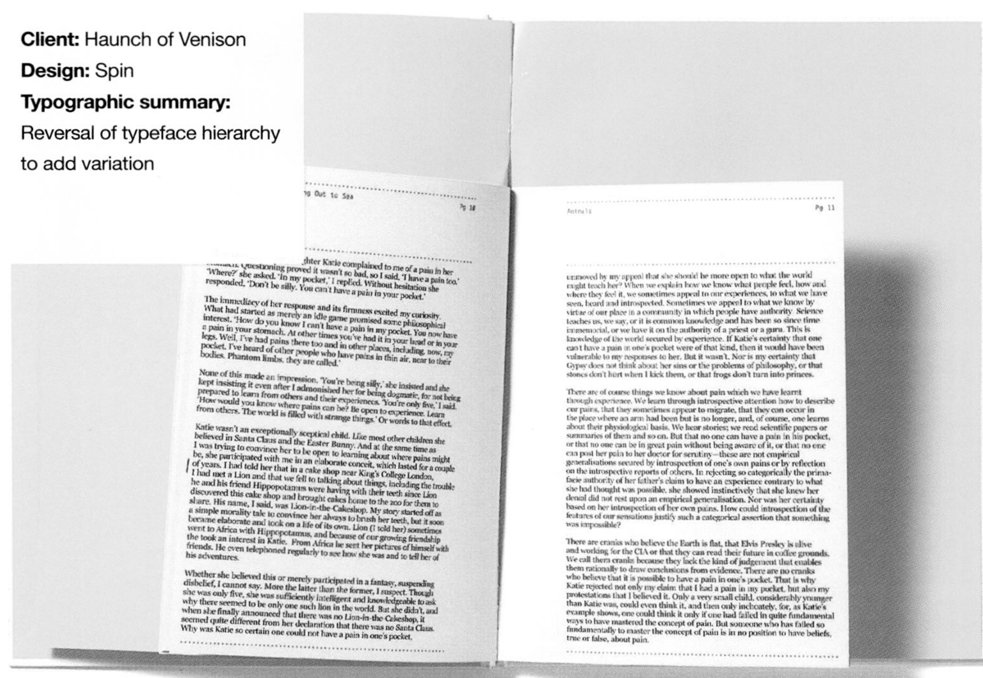

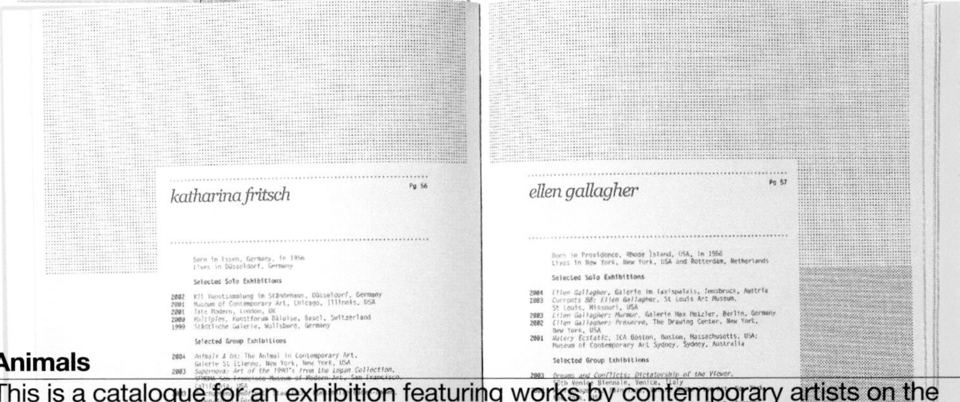

Animals

This is a catalogue for an exhibition featuring works by contemporary artists on the theme of animals. It has a smaller tipped-in brochure, which contains essays and biographies that accompanies the images. The tipped-in brochure uses multiple typefaces; Georgia Animals (a tweaked version of the system typeface Georgia), Letter Gothic Animals (again a tweaked version of a typeface) and Letter Gothic MT. Additional variation is gained by reversing the type usage in different sections of the catalogue. In the essays, for instance, Letter Gothic is used for the header, and Georgia Animals for the body text. In the biographies, an italicised Georgia Animals is used for the header and Letter Gothic used for body text.

Text hierarchy

Text hierarchy is a logical and visual guide, which allows the variety of headings that normally accompany body text to be organised. Hierarchy indicates different degrees of importance through the use of point sizes and/or type styles. It is important to note though that the use of a too complex text hierarchy can be distracting and reduces visual harmony.

This document, designed to promote the global identity of The Climate Group, is split into two brochures. The smaller one (this page), features a series of easily digestible sound-bite facts. The minimal typography and limited colour range with which they are presented, corresponds to the rather ominous nature of the content. The larger companion volume (facing page), carries greater detail, but retains the powerful qualities of the stark typography seen in the smaller brochure.

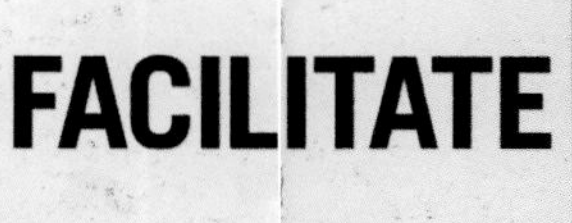

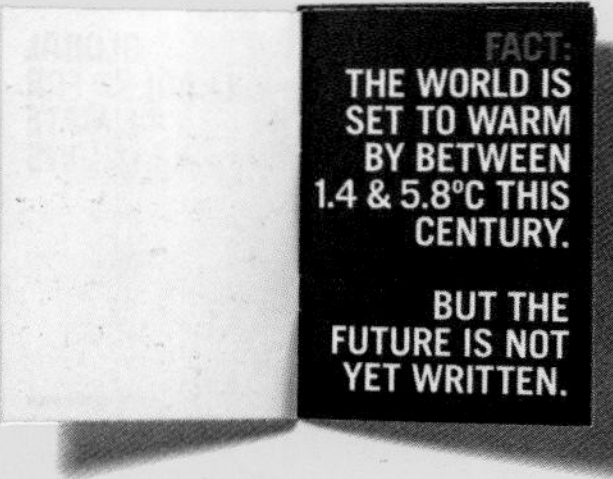

The Climate Group (above and opposite)

This global identity for The Climate Group, created by Browns, seeks to catalyse global action amongst governments and corporations to address the challenge of global climate change. The headings are set in the same upper case sans-serif typeface and point size (or smaller), as the body text. Text is differentiated by an effective use of colour.

Client: The Climate Group
Design: Browns
Typographic summary:
Simple text hierarchy with colour differentiation

FACT:
BETWEEN
1990 & 2000
INVESTING IN
ENERGY EFFICIENCY
ALLOWED DUPONT
TO HOLD ENERGY
USE FLAT WHILE
INCREASING
PRODUCTION
35% & SAVING
THE COMPANY
$2 BILLION.

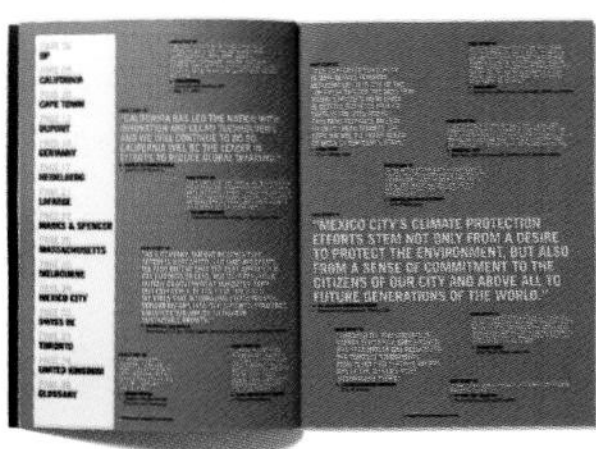

"IF WE DO NOT BEGIN NOW, MORE SUBSTANTIAL, MORE DISRUPTIVE AND MORE EXPENSIVE CHANGE WILL BE NEEDED LATER ON."

A head

The A head is the primary heading usually reserved for the title of a piece. It uses the largest point size – here it is shown in 14pt bold type – to indicate its predominance.

B head

The second hierarchy classification, the B head, has a smaller point size than an A head – here it is shown in 12pt type – but remains larger than that of body text. B heads usually include chapter headings.

C head

The C head may be the same point size as the body text, but could be differentiated by an italic or bold version of the typeface.

A head
A head in bold with spacing

B head
B head in regular with spacing

C head in body text, in italic and with no spacing

A head
A head in bold with spacing

B HEAD
B head in small caps

C head in body text, in italic and with no spacing

A head
A head in different colour to body text and in larger type size

B head
B head in different colour, larger type size but same weight as body text

C head in different colour, same point size and weight

Type on a page

Type on a page can be styled in a number of different ways; to ease or hinder readability, to convey a certain emotion, to relate to and enhance graphic elements or perhaps to create a unique sense of identity and space.

How text is set, and the space within which it is set, can have a dramatic effect on how easy it is to read and, on which part of the text grabs the attention of a reader first. This block is quite standard and is set 10pt type on 10pt leading.

Text set 10pt on 10pt.

This second block includes a 5mm indent, which creates an eye-catching space at the start of a paragraph.

Text set 10pt on 10pt with the inclusion of a 5mm indent.

This third piece uses a space to clearly demarcate a paragraph break.

A space of any size can be inserted sufficient for it to be noticeable (here it is + 2pt), but not exceeding a full line space as with the use of a full return.

Text set 10pt on 10pt with 2mm of space added after the first paragraph.

'With non-hanging punctuation the text appears to shift or be slightly indented, which can be distracting.'

This text block shows non-hanging punctuation such as quotation marks...

"With hanging punctuation the text appears as one single, solid block."

..and how the text block looks using hanging punctuation.

A different point size is not necessary to identify a title.
An emboldened version of a typeface creates sufficient difference to distinguish it from the body text.

This text block uses a hierarchy to distinguish levels of importance.

The grey bars highlight the leading spacing, which is measured from the left-hand margin of the text block to the right-hand margin and, which may or may not be where a line of ranged-left text ends.

In this text block, the 10pt type is set with additional leading (14pt) to open up more space between the lines.

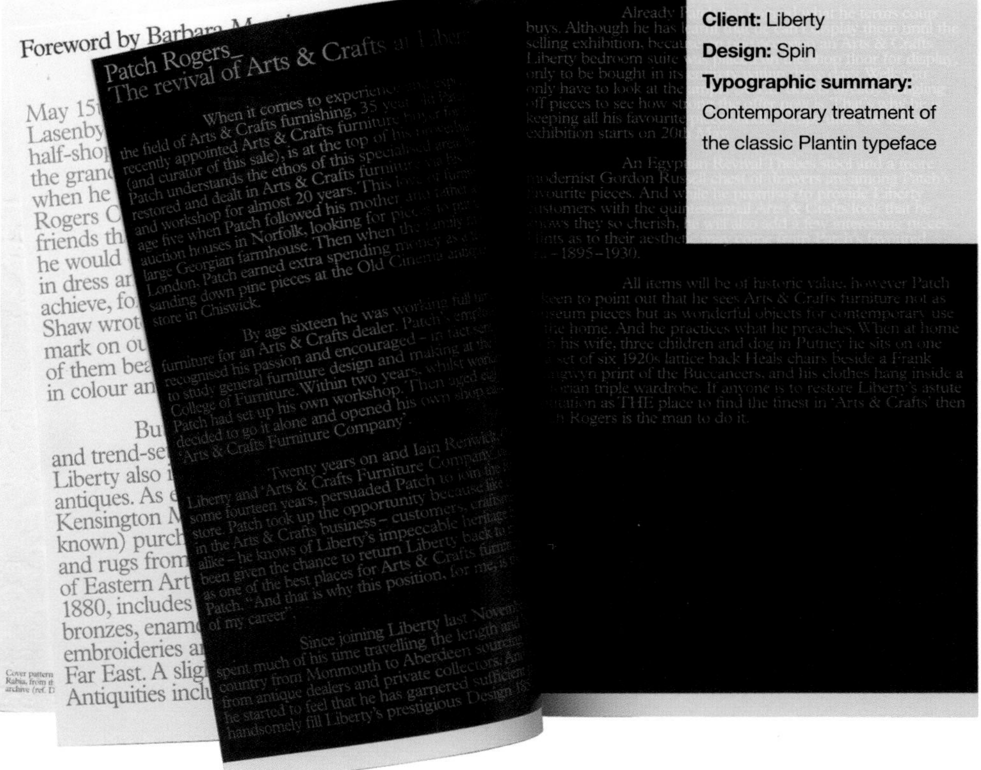

Client: Liberty
Design: Spin
Typographic summary: Contemporary treatment of the classic Plantin typeface

Liberty

This catalogue demonstrates that a contemporary feel can be achieved by using classic typefaces such as Plantin in a modern way. In this example, the indentation, leading and colour all contribute towards producing an elegant, yet contemporary appearance. Other modern interventions include the use of an underscore following the author's name and use of an indent that bites further into the paragraph than is the accepted norm. Here it is used with more classical proportions.

Indentation

An indentation is a space inserted between the left margin and the start of a text block. Text is typically indented to provide an entrance point to the paragraph that is easy to locate. The indentation point can be obtained in a number of ways, but is commonly determined when establishing the basic layout guidelines that form the space for the text block.

Type can be set using a variety of horizontal alignments, as demonstrated below. Alignment, when used effectively, can help harmonise text with other elements in the design, but large text blocks that are not left aligned or justified can become difficult and tiring to read as the eye loses its place.

A right-ranged text block can be
difficult to read as the starting place
for each line is irregular.

Range right, ragged left

Left-ranged text is commonplace. It is the
simplest alignment to read as each line
starts on the far left.

Range left, ragged right

Centred type is not commonly used for
body text as it also suffers from irregular starting
points for each line. It is often used for
headings and pull-quotes.

Centred

Justified text creates a neat text block with straight sides. This can introduce unsightly gaps between words as the lines are stretched to fill the measure, as shown in the second line here.

Justified

The gaps in justified blocks of text are easier to identify if you turn the text upside down. This prevents you from reading it, and therefore makes the gaps more obvious to the eye.

The gaps in the second line of inverted text stand out more sharply than in the third line of the same text block when viewed the right way up.

The gaps in the second line of inverted text stand out more sharply than in the third line of the same text block when viewed the right way up.

Client: Canongate Books
Design: Pentagram (Angus Hyland)
Typographic summary: Helvetica set in italic caps, various point sizes

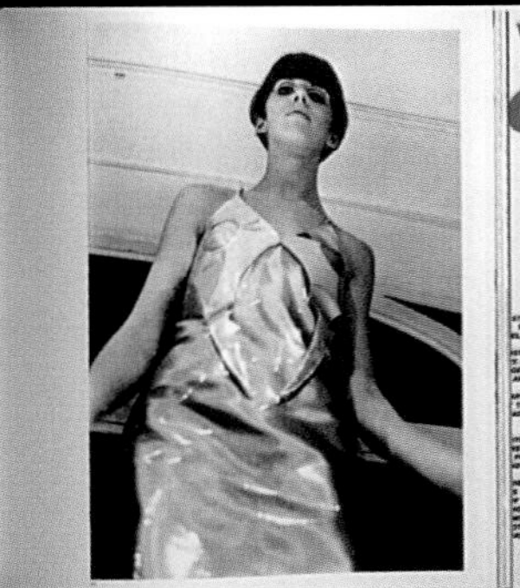

Andy Warhol: The Factory Years

Angus Hyland, partner at Pentagram, produced this design for *Andy Warhol: The Factory Years 1964–67* on behalf of Canongate Books. The volume is a collection of images and reflections by New York photographer Nat Finkelstein, who was the unofficial photographer at The Factory for more than two years.

The text, which describes Finkelstein's recollections and points of note, is set in a Helvetica sans-serif typeface. This is displayed in italic caps and the point size changes throughout the book to reflect the frenetic nature of the commentary provided.

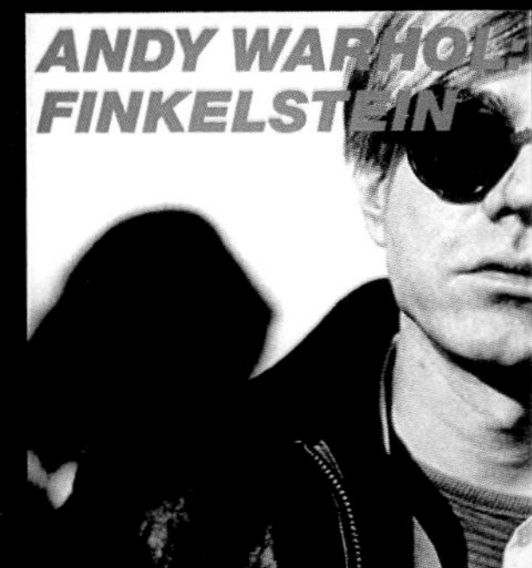

Numerals

There are two classifications of numerals: Old Style (or lower case), and Lining (or upper case). Lining numerals are aligned to the baseline and are all of equal height, whereas old style numerals do not, which means they can be difficult to read.

Lining numerals have characters with equal height and monospaced widths so that each numeral occupies exactly the same width as any other. This characteristic can often provide a great deal of additional display space, which it may be necessary to kern (or remove), particularly after the numeral '1'.

Lining (or upper case), numerals

Numerals, when set as Lining figures in body text – 5,452.16 for example – have a tendency to look oversized when compared to their old style counterparts. As the figures are of equal size to capital letters and occupy the same space – from baseline to cap height – they receive too much prominence in body text.

Old Style (or lower case), numerals

Old Style numerals – 5,452.16 – look in proportion to the lower case characters. The numbers 6 and 8 sit on the baseline and reach the cap height, while 1, 2 and 0 sit on the baseline and align to the x-height.

The remaining characters, 3, 4, 7 and 9 effectively have descenders that help to blend the numerals into body text.

Small capital numerals

SMALL CAPITAL VARIATIONS OF TYPEFACES ALSO HAVE OLD STYLE FIGURES – 5,452.16 – THIS HELPS THE NUMERALS BLEND WITH THE BODY TEXT.

IT IS WORTH REMEMBERING THAT GENERATING FAKE SMALL CAPS (AS SHOWN HERE), WILL OFTEN RESULT IN NUMERALS AND PUNCTUATION THAT APPEAR PROPORTIONALLY LARGER – 5,452.16.

Lining (or upper case), serif numerals

1234567890

Old Style (or lower case), serif numerals

1234567890

Sabon (top) Sabon Bold (bottom)

Sabon is a serif typeface that has both Lining and Old Style numeral variations.

Although the differences between these styles of numerals may appear subtle, they can alter the overall readability and appearance of numerical data. There are no hard and fast rules to numeral selection, indeed you may be limited due to the nature of the typography used elsewhere.

Sans-serif typefaces typically only carry a set of Lining numerals, while serif variations will often have both Lining and Old Style numerals. There are exceptions (see below), although certain typefaces may only be available in limited weights.

As a general guide, lining numerals work better in tabular matter as there are no ascenders or descenders to disrupt the flow of the eye. Old Style numerals are better suited to use within body text as their adjusted size and positioning is in harmony with the proportions of the lower case alphabet.

Lining (or upper case), sans-serif numerals

1234567890

Old Style (or lower case), sans-serif numerals

1234567890

Akzidenz Grotesk BE (top) Akzidenz Grotesk BE Light (bottom)

Akzidenz Grotesk is a sans-serif typeface that has both Old Style and Lining numeral variations.

Typesetting is about making choices, and good typesetting is about making the right choices. Even setting a simple column of numerals requires consideration. As with most examples in this book, a successful design rests upon a clear understanding of what the brief is attempting to achieve. These three examples of setting numerals (below), all have unique advantages and are used for specific reasons.

Right alignment

The numerals will right align in the column only if they have an equal number of characters before and after the decimal point. Any additional material, such as asterisks, daggers or double daggers, will shunt the text to the left. This makes the vertical alignment of characters irregular and greatly impinges legibility.

£12.50
221.73***†‡
124.76
£358.99

This system is useful when it's important to maintain an overall column pattern – i.e. that nothing protrudes from the line of the column.

Decimal and character alignment

Inevitably columns of numerals are irregular. Decimal and character alignment can compensate for this. By aligning on the pound sign and decimal point, all numerals align vertically and any additional characters are aligned to the right of the column. As these numerals aren't monospaced, the narrow number '1' is causing misalignment in previous numerals.

£ 12.50
221.73 ***†‡
124.76
£ 358.99

This system is useful when setting data that is accompanied by expanded footnotes.

Monospaced numerals

With monospaced numerals, each character and punctuation mark occupies an equal amount of space, and automatically align vertically. Highlighted in the diagram (right), the numbers '1' and '7', although different in character width, are equal in character space.

£ 12.50
221.73*
124.76
£ 358.99

This system is useful when setting data that is accompanied by expanded footnotes.

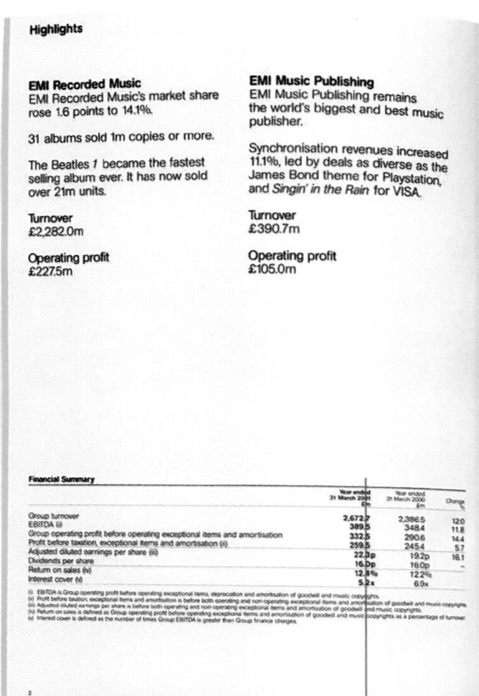

Highlights

EMI Recorded Music
EMI Recorded Music's market share rose 1.6 points to 14.1%.

31 albums sold 1m copies or more.

The Beatles *1* became the fastest selling album ever. It has now sold over 21m units.

Turnover
£2,282.0m

Operating profit
£227.5m

EMI Music Publishing
EMI Music Publishing remains the world's biggest and best music publisher.

Synchronisation revenues increased 11.1%, led by deals as diverse as the James Bond theme for Playstation, and *Singin' in the Rain* for VISA.

Turnover
£390.7m

Operating profit
£105.0m

Financial Summary

	Year ended 31 March 2001 £m	Year ended 31 March 2000 £m	Change %
Group turnover	2,672.7	2,386.5	12.0
EBITDA (i)	389.5	348.4	11.8
Group operating profit before operating exceptional items and amortisation	332.5	290.6	14.4
Profit before taxation, exceptional items and amortisation (ii)	259.5	245.4	5.7
Adjusted diluted earnings per share (iii)	22.3p	19.2p	16.1
Dividends per share	16.0p	16.0p	–
Return on sales (iv)	12.4%	12.2%	
Interest cover (v)	5.2x	6.9x	

(i) EBITDA is Group operating profit before operating exceptional items, depreciation and amortisation of goodwill and music copyrights.
(ii) Profit before taxation, exceptional items and amortisation is before both operating and non-operating exceptional items and amortisation of goodwill and music copyrights.
(iii) Adjusted diluted earnings per share is before both operating and non-operating exceptional items and amortisation of goodwill and music copyrights.
(iv) Return on sales is defined as Group operating profit before operating exceptional items and amortisation of goodwill and music copyrights as a percentage of turnover.
(v) Interest cover is defined as the number of times Group EBITDA is greater than Group finance charges.

2

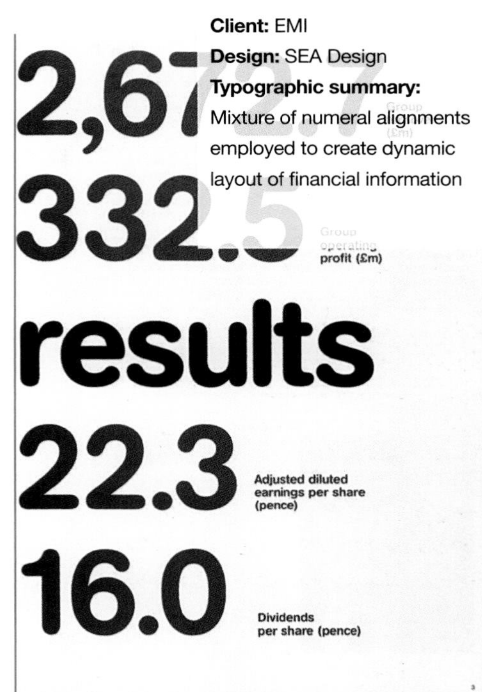

2,672.7
332.5
Group operating profit (£m)
results
22.3
Adjusted diluted earnings per share (pence)
16.0
Dividends per share (pence)
3

Client: EMI
Design: SEA Design
Typographic summary:
Mixture of numeral alignments employed to create dynamic layout of financial information

Decimal alignment
These figures are conventionally aligned on the decimal point, allowing additional symbols to be included without breaking the vertical harmony that the figures naturally create.

Left alignment
Here graphic figures align left, and related units are reproduced much in a smaller point size in the copy that sits to the right. Although unconventional, this makes a clear and dynamic layout that emphasises the value of the figures.

EMI

Annual reports and financial literature require specific attention to the way in which numerals are set. This annual report for EMI by SEA Design uses a mixture of alignments to create an engaging design focusing on the clear bold use of figures. The cover of this brochure can be seen on page 127.

Tabular
Tabular matter is a term applied to any information that is presented in table format, whether it is quantitative numerical content, such as statistics and company results, or qualitative textual information.

Drop and standing capitals

A drop capital (or drop cap), is a design feature whereby the initial letter of the first word in a paragraph is set in a larger point size, and aligned with the top of the first line of text. The drop cap might be an ornate typeface as in medieval illuminated manuscripts, or something simpler that may have the body text wrapped around it.

Drop caps are eye-catching elements that can dramatically affect the appearance of a text block depending on their point size and the number of text lines they occupy.

hen using drop caps, the first letter of the body text must be removed so that it is not repeated. Where possible, you should avoid using any word that will form a new word if the first letter is removed. For example, 'She' becomes 'S he'. Finally, you should avoid using a drop cap for a word that only has two letters.

Theoretically, a drop cap can occupy any number of text lines. However, you should take into account the measure of the block in which it will be placed so that it does not result in an unbalanced or uneven look.

Not nearly as common as the drop cap, the standing capital is also a typesetting alternative. It sits on the same baseline as the rest of the text yet without the body text stacking up against it as is seen with a drop cap. When used, care needs to be taken to ensure that the text is sufficiently kerned so as not to create a typographical distraction.

Client: The Logan Collection

Design: Aufuldish + Warinner

Typographic summary: Large, green, bracketed capital, overprinted with body text

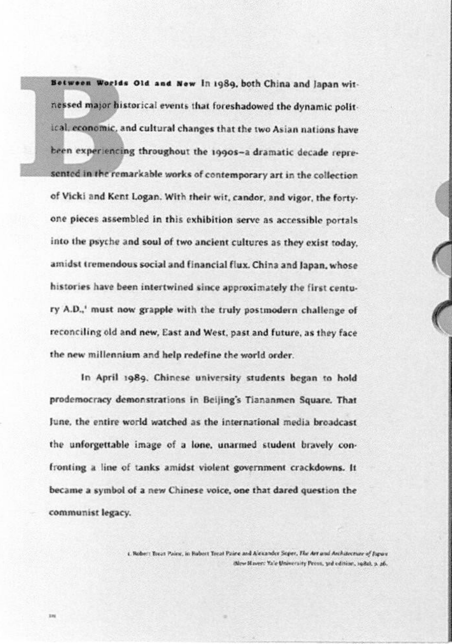

Between Worlds Old and New In 1989, both China and Japan witnessed major historical events that foreshadowed the dynamic political, economic, and cultural changes that the two Asian nations have been experiencing throughout the 1990s–a dramatic decade represented in the remarkable works of contemporary art in the collection of Vicki and Kent Logan. With their wit, candor, and vigor, the forty-one pieces assembled in this exhibition serve as accessible portals into the psyche and soul of two ancient cultures as they exist today, amidst tremendous social and financial flux. China and Japan, whose histories have been intertwined since approximately the first century A.D.,[1] must now grapple with the truly postmodern challenge of reconciling old and new, East and West, past and future, as they face the new millennium and help redefine the world order.

In April 1989, Chinese university students began to hold prodemocracy demonstrations in Beijing's Tiananmen Square. That June, the entire world watched as the international media broadcast the unforgettable image of a lone, unarmed student bravely confronting a line of tanks amidst violent government crackdowns. It became a symbol of a new Chinese voice, one that dared question the communist legacy.

1. Robert Treat Paine, in Robert Treat Paine and Alexander Soper, *The Art and Architecture of Japan* (New Haven: Yale University Press, 3rd edition, 1981), p. 26.

The Logan Collection

This is a catalogue published by The Logan Collection of Vale, Colorado, USA to celebrate its tenth anniversary of collecting contemporary art. The catalogue features a collection of essays and installation photographs from works in the collection. Aufuldish + Warinner overprinted large, green, bracketed capitals with body text to imitate drop caps and form a focal point on the text pages. Although it is overprinted, the capital still fulfils its function of leading the eye to the start of the text block.

Special characters

Letterforms and numerals alone are not sufficient to structure comprehensive textural information, or communicate phonetic stresses and the infinite number of ideas and propositions that we wish to.

In order to satisfy this function we need various special characters. Punctuation enables us to qualify, quantify and organise information; accents provide us with information about how a letter is stressed or sounds; and pictograms provide shorthand information. The examples shown below, while not exhaustive, introduce all the major characters that, if correctly used, can enhance a design.

All typefaces are not equal
Most typefaces contain punctuation and miscellaneous characters but not all carry a comprehensive range of both. Graphic typefaces tend to have fewer special characters and it is worth exploring this before selecting a typeface for a design. Additional characters may not be required for all jobs but for some, a reduced set of special characters could be problematic. Pump (below), has a limited set of additional characters, while Centaur (bottom), comes with a complete set including accented small caps and swashes.

!"$&'()*,-./:;\]ÄÇÑÜààâäãåçéèêíìîïñóòôöõúùûü¢£•ß´¨ÆØ¥œø¿i ƒ

«»...ÀÃÕœ-—""''ÿŸ/‹›fifl·„‰Â ÊÁËÈÍÎÏÌÓÔÒÚÛÙıˆ˜¯˚

!"#$%&'()*+,-/:;<=>?@[\]^_`{|}~ÄÅÇÉÑÖÜáàâäãåçéèêëíìîïñóòôöõúùûü†

°¢£§•¶ß®©™´¨≠ÆØ∞±≤≥¥µ∂∑∏π∫ªºΩæø¿¡¬√ƒ≈∆«»…ÀÃÕŒœ——""

''÷◊ÿŸ/¤‹›fifl‡·‚„‰‰ÂÊÁËÈÍÎÏÌÓÔÒÚÛÙıˆ˜¯˘˙˚¸˝˛ˇ!¢$$& ()…,-.Ð¼½¾⅛⅜⅝⅓

⅔Rfffiflffiffl()^-`₡IRp~a¢ÁÀÂÄÃÅÇÉÈÊËÍÌÎÏÑÓÒÔÖÕÚÙÛÜ8 43687Š¢2¨ˇo5Ý$Þ90ŽÆØ¿1Ł)),Œ—¯i

Ÿ1234567 90erdl ¸˘-bnm,,·° && ABCDEFGHIJKLMNOPQRSTUVWXYZaeteqkspsttvwz

The London Institute Gallery

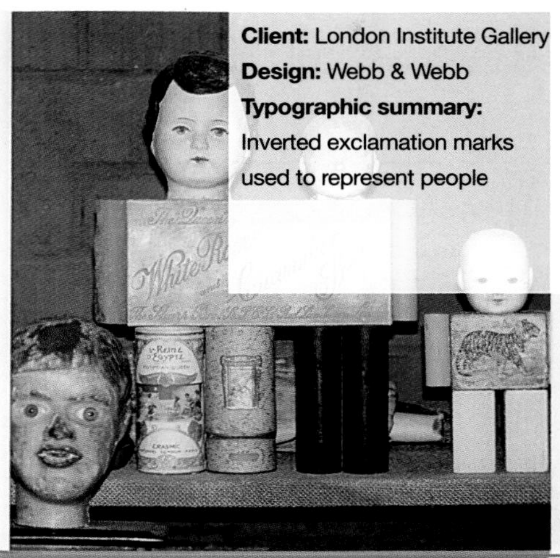

Client: London Institute Gallery
Design: Webb & Webb
Typographic summary:
Inverted exclamation marks used to represent people

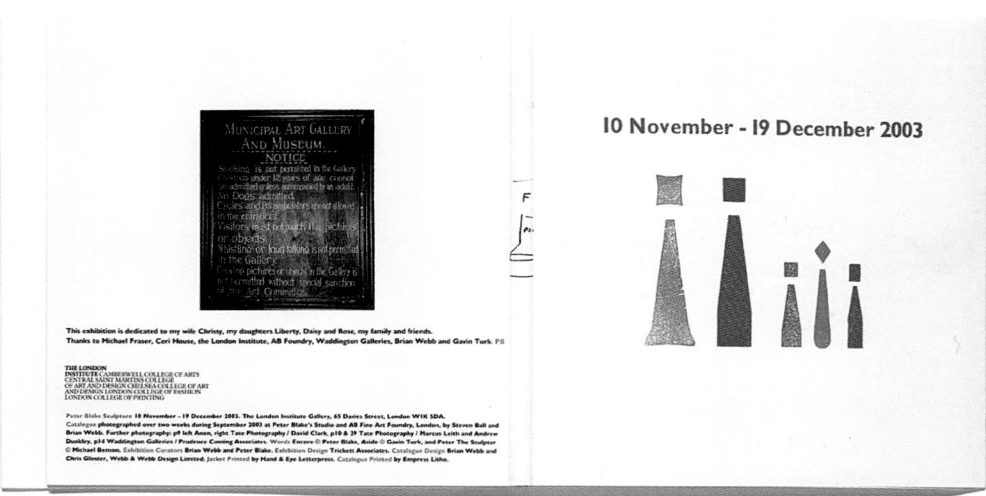

London Institute Gallery

Webb & Webb designed this guide for an exhibition of sculptor Peter Blake's work, held at the London Institute Gallery. The brochure uses inverted exclamation marks to mirror the shape of Blake's sculptures. The exclamation marks resemble people and reflect individual personalities and different textures via the wood-block printing method used. The family of exclamation marks grows on successive pages, initially starting with two members, then increasing to four and so on.

Ligatures

A ligature is a typographical device that joins two or three separate characters together to form a single unit. They are used as a solution to the interference that certain character combinations create. Ligatures are formed either by extending the crossbar or connecting the ascenders depending upon the characters involved.

The term ligature is derived from 'Ligare', which is the Latin word for 'bind'. A ligature may also be used to represent a specific sound such as the capital Æ diphthong. Interestingly the ampersand character (&), is a ligature of the Latin word 'et', which means 'and'.

Lower case combinations

The ascender of the 'f' character and the serif belonging to the ascender of a following character can sometimes look as if they are interfering with each other. Rather than trying to separate them through use of kerning, they are often joined by a ligature (as shown below). Similarly, where the dot of the 'i' or 'j' can appear cumbersome when following the 'f', a ligature that joins at the crossbar can be used, and the dot is removed.

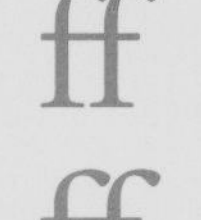

ff fi fl ffi ffl

ﬀ ﬁ ﬂ ﬃ ﬄ

Dante / Dante Expert

Pictured above left are the standard characters and, shown below left, with their replacement ligatures. The 'i' loses its dot and the arms of the 'ff' join in one continuous crossbar.

Upper case combinations

For the same reasons as outlined above, ligatures are also used in pairs of certain capitals

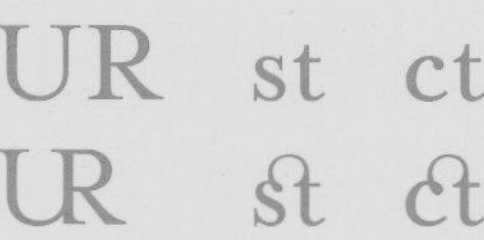

VA TW TY UR st ct

Mrs Eaves

The lower case letters (left) show that a ligature can be added for letter pairs, in order to introduce extra creative flourishes.

University of Sussex

This prospectus for the University of Sussex, designed by Blast design studio features a ligature joining the institution's initials and forms part of a new identity for the university.

An amended version of Baskerville was cut for the prospectus, and is also used as the header typeface and for campus signage. This new version is far more dynamic than the more formal original version (shown on page 42), which has double terminals at the foot of the letters. The amended Baskerville has a single terminal on lower case ascenders such as 'h' and a round foot on the 'm' for example. The rounding of the new cut is used as a key component of the university's logo ligature.

Client: University of Sussex

Design: Blast

Typographic summary: Ligature-based logotype and amended Baskerville typeface create a unifying identity

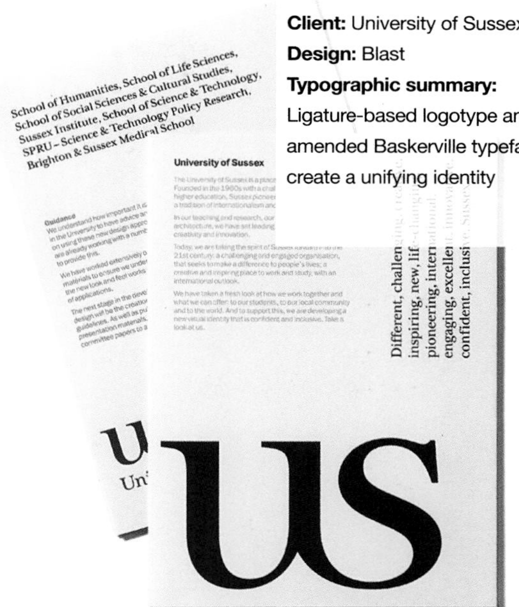

abcdefghijklmnopqrstuvwxyz
ABCDEFGHIJKLMNOPQRST
UVWXYZ 1234567890

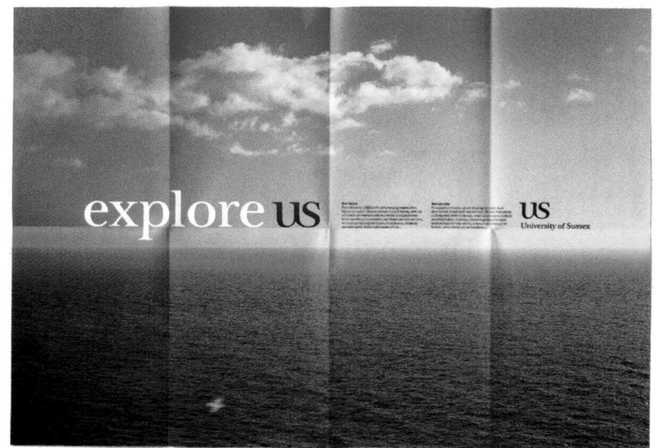

The poster combines the simplified typography with an open, aspirational image within which the central prominence of the ligature suggests inclusiveness and connection.

The right character for the job

A typeface usually contains a suite of supporting characters, some of which are demonstrated below:

Typographic quotation marks (curly quotes) and primes

These two examples (below left), are single and double quotation marks. It is a common mistake to use primes (below right), instead of the correct 'curly quotes'. The single prime is used to denote inches, minutes or point size. The double prime is used to denote feet and hours.

‘Single’ “Double” 'Single' "Double"

British-English conventions

Knowing which is the correct character for a job is only half the problem as you also need to understand the different usage conventions. Confusingly American and English settings are the opposite of each other. In British English, the primary quotation mark is the single mark, while a quote within this uses double quotation marks. Punctuation sits outside the secondary quotation marks (see below) clarifying that the punctuation is not part of the quote.

‘I said “that’s not right”, but no one listened’

American-English conventions

In American English the opposite is true: double quotation marks are used for the primary quote, with single quotation marks used for the secondary. Punctuation falls inside these secondary quotation marks.

“I said ‘that’s not right,’ but no one listened”

The dotless ‘i’

The dotless ‘i’ is supplied with most typefaces. Although strictly speaking it is not a ligature, it performs a similar function. Often used in advertising copy where space can be restricted, the dotless ‘i’ tucks under an over-hanging character such as the arm of a ‘T’.

i ı Tight Tıght

Accents

Most typefaces are supplied with common accents: acutes (á, é, í, ó, ú), grave (à, è, ì, ò, ù), cedilla (ç), umlauts or dieresis (ä, ë, ï, ö, ü), circumflex (â, ê, î, ô, û), ring (å) and tilde (ã). You may have noticed that typefaces often contain accents as individual characters (1). These can be used with letters (2), to create accented characters by kerning them together. The resulting characters (3) are regularly used in Polish, but are not available in standard character sets, but this technique provides a solution.

1 **˙ ¸**

2 **˙z c¸**

3 **ż ç**

Client: Swiss RE CfGD
Design: Frost Design
Typographic summary: Quotation marks used as an iconic image

Swiss RE CfGD

This identity for reinsurance company Swiss RE's Centre for Global Dialogue by Frost Design studio uses quotation marks as an iconic symbol to represent dialogue. This punctuation character is used over the range of literature and print pieces that were produced for the organisation. In the example pictured it is used as a subtle tone on tone, but at a scale that fills the page.

The Centre for Global Dialogue provides a forum to deal with global risk issues and to facilitate new insight into future risk markets.

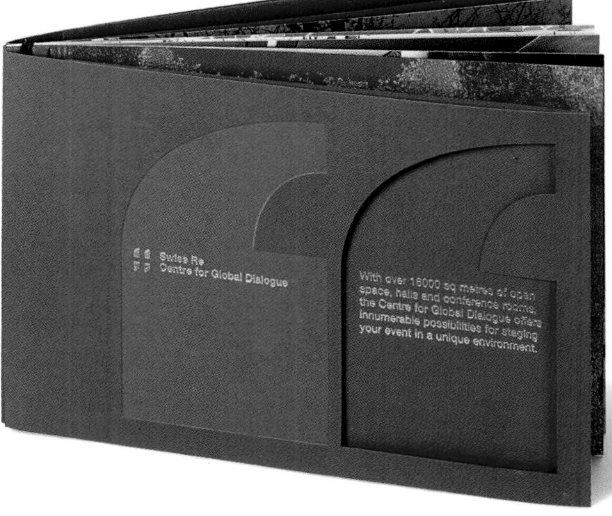

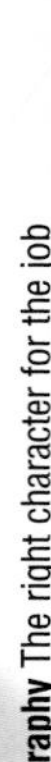

Punctuation

Punctuation usage and marks can vary significantly in a number of west European languages, as these examples demonstrate.

French conventions

Guillemets are used in French in place of speech marks. As with British English, any punctuation sits outside of the guillemets. Note, that unlike British English, a space is inserted around the text being quoted. Other characters are also preceded by a space.

Traditionally, « guillemets », are used in place of speech marks in written French.

10 % No ! When ? Reference † Em dashes— Colons: Semi-colons;

Italian conventions

Guillemets are used in Italian as they are in French.

The ellipsis indicating a break in speech…. is a four-dot version, set close up.

Spanish conventions

Spanish typographic conventions are similar to French, although there are some differences.

«for quotations guillemets are usually used»

¡An inverted exclamation mark starts a sentence that is exclamatory such as giving an order, and a normal exclamation mark ends it!

¿An interrogatory sentence begins with an inverted question mark and ends with a normal question mark?

Em dashes— are set closed up to the parenthetical part of the sentence, and followed by a word space

German conventions

German quote marks come in a variety of forms. Em dashes are treated as in British English.

«there are several conventions for quotations in German. Here guillemets are used»

»these can be reversed«

„or double primes, or double speech marks can be used. If this is the case they are reversed with the opening quotation mark aligned on the baseline and the closing one aligned top“

Em dashes — are followed and preceded by a standard word space.

Client: Black Dog Publishing

Design: Gavin Ambrose

Typographic summary:

Dual-language book with guillemets and speech marks

In the Park II (incident on the Quai de Morges), 1978

Dans le parc II, (incident sur le quai de Morges), 1978

176

is only witnessed purely through the impure speech of blasphemy, will not cease to be indissociably bound [illegible]

Where does this power come from, this power that is in one sense the most mysterious, the least avowable? Is it second? Is it first? Though non-identical, is it not the same as the Sovereign Power? And if the Other has always been what represents evil, its place or its spirit, will we not perceive, through a discovery that will shake us, that [illegible] Same, although non-identical, insofar, therefore, as the Other being the same, denounces in this way the non-identity of the Same? From which the infinite consequences, not only as for the declaration of "last questions" and what one calls the spiritual domain, but as far as in our logic, in which the calm principle of identity suddenly finds itself disparaged, without, however, surrendering its place to the no less calm principle of contrariety, such as invoked by dialectic. For the negative (let us call it the "spiritual power of malice") no longer consists in what is opposed to the same, but in pure similitude, in minute distance and imperceptible separation, not even in the deception of imitation (which always pays homage to the portrait), but in this strange principle, namely, that there, where there are likenesses, there are an

D'où vient cette puissance, en un sens la plus mystérieuse, la moins avouable? Est-elle seconde, est-elle première? N'est-elle pas, encore que non identique, la même que la Souveraine Puissance? Et si l'Autre est depuis toujours ce qui représente le mal, son lieu ou son esprit, n'allons-nous pas apercevoir, par une découverte qui va nous ébranler, que l'Autre n'est autre que dans la mesure où il est le Même, encore que non identique, dans la mesure donc où, l'Autre étant le même, il dénonce par là la non-identité du Même ? D'où des conséquences infinies, non seulement quant à l'énoncé des « questions dernières » et ce que l'on appelle le domaine spirituel, mais jusque dans notre logique où le tranquille principe d'identité va tout à coup se trouver battu en brèche, sans pourtant céder la place au non moins tranquille principe de contrariété tel que l'invoque la dialectique. Car le négatif (appelons-le la « puissance spirituelle de méchanceté ») n'est plus dans ce qui s'oppose au même, mais dans la pure similitude, dans la distance infime et l'écart insensible, non pas même dans la tromperie de la contrefaçon (qui rend toujours hommage au portrait), mais dans cet étrange principe, à savoir que, là où il y a des semblables, il y a une infinité de semblables et, là où l'infini scintille dans la pluralité des distincts indiscernables, l'image doit cesser d'être seconde par rapport à un prétendu premier objet et doit

177

origin, is the force of repetition; which never says "once and for all" but "yet again", "this has already taken place once and will take place once again, and always again, and again". Whence the great burst of laughter that is the shudder of the universe, the opening of space in its seriousness, and divine humour *par excellence*. Because the eternal return even in the oblivion in which its revelation as law culminates, – this eternal return in which the infinite absence of the gods is affirmed and in some way proved – must also come to desire the return of the gods, that is, the gods as return. This is what Pierre Klossowski expounds in a superb development that I would like to cite partially here, because it accounts for not only Nietzsche but, it seems to me, Klossowski too:

> And thus it appears that the doctrine of eternal return is conceived yet again as a *simulacrum of doctrine* whose very parodic character accounts for *hilarity* as an attribute of existence sufficient unto itself, when laughter bursts from the depths of the whole truth, either because truth explodes in the laughter of the gods, or because the gods themselves die from uncontrollable laughter. When a god wanted to be the only God, all the other gods were seized by uncontrollable laughter, until they *died* from laughter.

fois pour toutes », mais: « encore une autre fois » , « cela a déjà eu lieu une fois et aura lieu encore une fois, et toujours à nouveau, à nouveau ». D'où l'immense éclat de rire qui est le frisson de l'univers, l'ouverture de l'espace en son sérieux et l'humeur divine par excellence. Car il faut bien que l'éternel retour, jusque dans l'oubli où culmine sa révélation comme loi, cet éternel retour où s'affirme et en quelque sorte se prouve l'absence infinie des dieux, en vienne à vouloir aussi le retour des dieux, c'est-à-dire les dieux comme retour. Ce que Pierre Klossowski expose en un développement superbe que je voudrais citer partiellement ici, parce qu'il rend compte, non seulement de Nietzsche, mais, il me semble, de Klossowski.

> Et ainsi apparaît que la doctrine de l'éternel retour se conçoit encore une fois comme un *simulacre de doctrine* dont le caractère parodique même rend compte de l'*hilarité* comme attribut de l'existence se suffisant à elle-même, lorsque le rire éclate au fond de l'entière vérité, soit que la vérité explose dans le rire des dieux, soit que les dieux eux-mêmes meurent de fou rire: Quand un dieu voulut être le seul Dieu, tous les autres dieux furent pris de fou rire, jusqu'à mourir de rire.

A sentence that, precisely, will constitute one of the leitmotivs of *Le Baphomet* and that holds in its simplicity the endless movement of truth in the error of its return. Otherwise, why this laughter? Because of the divine, yes: "what is the divine if not the fact that there are several gods and not God alone?" But in laughter, the gods die, thus confirming the risible pretension of One God (who does not laugh); however, dying of laughter, they make laughter divinity itself, "the supreme manifestation of the divine", where, if they disappear, it is to be reabsorbed, waiting to be reborn from it. Yet still, not everything has been said definitively for, if the gods die laughing, it is doubtless because laughter is the movement of the divine, but also because it is the very space of dying – dying and laughing, laughing divinely and laughing mortally, laughter as bacchic movement of the truth and laughter as mockery of the infinite error passing incessantly into one another. And thus everything returns to the absolute ambiguity of the unique sign that, wanting to divulge itself, looks for its equivalences and, finding them, loses itself in them and, losing itself, believes it finds itself.[5]

Phrase qui précisément va constituer l'un des leitmotive du *Baphomet* et qui détient dans sa simplicité le mouvement sans fin de la vérité dans l'erreur de son retour. Car, pourquoi ce rire ? Parce que le divin, oui, « qu'est-ce que le divin, sinon le fait qu'il y a plusieurs dieux et non pas Dieu seul? ». Mais, dans le rire, les dieux meurent, confirmant ainsi la risible prétention du Dieu Un (qui ne rit pas); cependant, mourant de rire, ils font du rire la divinté même, « la suprême manifestation du divin » où s'ils disparaissent, c'est pour se réabsorber, en attendant d'en renaître. Toutefois, tout n'est pas alors dit définitivement; car, s'ils meurent, les dieux, de rire, c'est sans doute que le rire est le mouvement du divin, mais c'est qu'il est aussi l'espace même de mourir – mourir et rire, rire divinement et rire mortellement, rire comme mouvement bachique du vrai et rire comme la risée de l'erreur infinie passant incessamment l'un dans l'autre. Et ainsi tout retourne à l'absolue ambiguïté du signe unique qui, voulant se divulguer, cherche ses équivalences et, les trouvant, s'y perd et, se perdant, croit se trouver.[5]

Decadence of the Nude / La décadence du Nu

These are pages from a dual-language book about Pierre Klossowski. 'Double-decker' text blocks are, wherever possible, kept aligned and this visually links the text blocks. This can be seen in the parallel running of indentations.

Non-alphabetical typefaces (or Pi fonts)

These are made entirely of graphic characters and may include scientific symbols, arrows, shapes and icons. The main use for these symbols is to add additional ideograms and flexibility into legends or body text, as shown below.

☎ to describe a service
✈ as a picture
☞ to point the way
✹ as a symbol
❾ as a number in a list
❏ as a shape

✡✢✣✤✥✦✧★☆✪✫✬✭✮✯✰✱✲✳✴✵✶✷✸✹✺

Zapf Dingbats

An ever popular set of symbols.

Woodtype Ornaments

A set of symbols inspired by woodtype blocks including several ‘printers hands’.

Restart

A series of hand drawn, sketch-like symbols.

International

A collection of common symbols in general use.

Braille

A standard alphabet that is read by touch, groups of dots are used to represent the letters.

Client: Self-published
Design: Gavin Ambrose and Matt Lumby
Typographic summary: Letters replaced with binary code

American Psycho Binary

This version of *American Psycho* by Brett Eastern Ellis was created by Gavin Ambrose and Matt Lumby. In this edition of the book the letterforms have been reproduced in binary code. Each letter of the work has been replaced by an eight-digit binary code. A consequence of this is that the book contains eight times as many characters, and so the book runs to over 1200 pages. Individual words also have extended lengths so that in many cases only one word will fit to a line.

Non-Latin typefaces

Due to the impact of globalisation and multinationals, designs that are produced for international markets will increasingly include text in non-Latin languages.

This has implications for spacing requirements for any given text block as the following examples demonstrate. In all the translations that appear on this page and the facing page, keywords and punctuation marks are highlighted in magenta. This demonstrates how familiar typographic differences are dealt with in different non-Latin languages.

Any given word is likely to alter its length as it is translated from one language into another. A designer should ensure that the type block, or space allocated for a piece of text, should be large enough to accommodate the additional space that the translated text requires.

This paragraph demonstrates the different space requirements for the same text in different languages. Translation into non-Latin languages, as the following examples show, has a far more significant impact on a design than the translation of Latin languages. **Emboldened** or *italicised* type can be successfully assimilated in most languages although typeface selection can be restricted. "Punctuation" usage varies, and the inclusion of symbols & marks aren't always what you'd expect!

Hebrew

פסקה זו מדגימה את דרישות הריווח השונות עבור אותן שורות טקסט כשהן מוצגות בשפות שונות.
כפי שניתן לראות מהדוגמאות הר"מ, תרגום טקסט לשפות לא-לטיניות משפיע על העיצוב בצורה משמעותית הרבה יותר מאשר תרגום טקסט לשפות לטיניות. ניתן לשלב בהצלחה טקסט **מודגש** או *נטוי* ברוב השפות, אם כי מגוון הגופנים עלול להיות מוגבל. השימוש ב"סימני פיסוק" משתנה משפה לשפה, ושילוב סמלים וסימנים אינו תמיד כפי שהייתם מצפים.

Arabic

هـــذه الفقـــرة تبيـــن المتطلبات المختلفة للمســـافة بين ســـطور النـــص عنـــد عرضهـــا بلغـــات مختلفة.
كما أن ترجمة النص إلى اللغات الغير لاتينية، كما يتبين فـــي الأمثلة التالية، إنما لهـــا أثر ملموس بصـــورة واضحة على تصميم الصفحة إذا قورن بترجمة النـــص باللغات اللاتينية. ويمكن بنجاح محاكاة الحروف **بلون داكن** أو *بأحرف مائلة* في معظم اللغـــات على الرغم مـــن أن إختيار نـــوع الحرف أو الفونت قد يكون محدوداً. ويختلف إســـتعمال «النقط والفواصل وما شـــابه»، كما أن إدخال الرموز والعلامات ليس دائما كما تتوقعونه!

Urdu

یہ پیراگراف اس بات کا مظہر ھے کہ ایک ھی مضمون کو جب مختلف زُبانوں میں ترجمہ کیا جاتا ھے تو اُس کے لیے مختلف جگہ کی ضرورت ھوتی ھے۔
کسی مضمون کا غیر لاطینی زُبانوں میں ترجمہ، جیسا کہ مندرجہ ذیل مثالوں سے ظاہر ہے، دوسری لاطینی زبانوں میں ترجمہ کے مقابلے میں تحریر کی وضع پر کہیں زیادہ اثر انداز ہوتا ہے۔ **جلی** یا *ثلث* (*ترچھی*) طرزِ تحریر کو بیشتر زبانوں میں کامیابی سے استعمال جا سکتا ہے اگرچہ ہو سکتا ہے کہ طرزِ تحریر کی اقسام محدود ہوں۔ "رموزِ اوقاف" کا استعمال مختلف ہوتا ہے اور علامات اور نشانات ہمیشہ وہ نہیں ہوتے ہیں جن کی آپ توقع کرتے ہوں۔

Korean

이 문단은 서로 언어로 되어 있는 동일한 내용의 서로 다른 공간 요구사항을 보여 준다. 다음 예들이 보여 주듯이 비라틴계 언어로 번역하는 것은 라틴계 언어의 번역보다 디자인에 훨씬 더 중대한 영향을 준다. 서체 선택이 제한적일 수 있는데도 **진하게 표시된** 또는 *이탤릭체* 로 표시된 글자는 대부분의 언어에서 성공적으로 동화될 수 있다. ″구두점″ 사용법은 서로 다르며 기호와 표시의 삽입도 언제나 예상과 다르다!

Cryllic

Данный абзац является иллюстрацией того, как меняются потребности в свободном месте для размещения одного и того же текста в зависимости от языка.
Переводы текста на языки с не латинским алфавитом, как показывает следующий пример, требуют более серьезных изменений дизайна страниц, чем переводы на языки с латинским алфавитом. Выделение **жирным шрифтом** или *курсивом* возможно для большинства языков, но выбор гарнитур для некоторых языков может быть ограниченным. Существуют также различия в знаках «пунктуации», а если используются специальные знаки и символы, они не всегда будут выглядеть так, как вы ожидаете!

Greek

Αυτή η παράγραφος αποτελεί δείγμα της διαφορετικής έκτασης που καταλαμβάνει το ίδιο κείμενο σε διαφορετικές γλώσσες.
Η μετάφραση κειμένων σε γλώσσες μη λατινογενείς, όπως αποδεικνύουν τα παρακάτω παραδείγματα, επηρεάζει πολύ περισσότερο το σχεδιασμό απ' ό,τι η μετάφραση κειμένων σε λατινογενείς γλώσσες.
Στις περισσότερες γλώσσες υπάρχει αντιστοιχία σε ό,τι αφορά τους **έντονους** ή *πλάγιους* χαρακτήρες, ενώ οι επιλογές γραμματοσειρών ενδέχεται να είναι περιορισμένες. Η χρήση των σημείων «στίξης» διαφέρει και τα σύμβολα και τα σημεία στίξης που χρησιμοποιούνται δεν είναι πάντα τα αναμενόμενα!

Chinese Traditional

這段文字顯示了同一內容在翻譯成不同語文後，所需的空間有所不同。就如以下例子證明，與翻譯成拉丁係語文比較，將文字翻譯成非拉丁文係語文對設計的影響比較大。雖然在許多語文中不難使用**黑體**或*斜體*，但是版面的選擇可能會比較少。此外，在不同語文中所使用的［標點符號］也有差異，所以您可能會有意想不到的符號與標記！

Chinese Simplified

这段文字显示了同一内容在翻译成不同语文后，所需的空间有所不同。就如以下例子证明，与翻译成拉丁系语文比较，将文字翻译成非拉丁文系语文对设计的影响比较大。虽然在许多语文中不难使用**黑体**或*斜体*，但是版面的选择可能会比较少。此外，在不同语文中所使用的［标点符号］也有差异，所以您可能会有意想不到的符号与标记！

Japanese

このパラグラフは、同じテキストを異なる言語で示す場合は異なった空白の仕方が必要です。次の例が示すように、ラテン語以外の言語へ翻訳する場合、文章のデザインにおいてラテン語の翻訳よりもはるかに大きな影響が現れます。書体選択には制限がありますが、**太文字**や*イタリック体*の文字はほとんどの言語書体において十分に整合します。"句読法"の用法はさまざまですが、記号やマークを使用しても必ずしも期待ほどの効果はありません！

Leading

Leading is a hot-metal printing term that refers to the strips of lead that were inserted between text measures in order to space them accurately. Leading is specified in points and refers nowadays to the space in between the lines of a text block. Leading introduces space into the text block and allows the characters to 'breathe' so that the information is easy to read.

To achieve a balanced and well-spaced text block, leading usually has a larger point size than the text it is associated with, for example a 12pt typeface might be set with 14pt leading.

8pt type on 8pt leading (set solid)

These text blocks demonstrate how the size of the leading affects the ability to read the text, and how it also affects the overall visual appearance.

Text set 8pt on 8pt is a very tight configuration.

8pt type on 9pt leading (set +1)

Text set 8pt on 9pt introduces more space between the text lines although it is still congested.

8pt type on 10pt leading (set +2)

Text set 8pt on 10pt is the optimal configuration in these examples, as it provides sufficient space between lines for the text to be easily read.

8pt type on 12pt leading (set +4)

The use of 12pt leading is too much for an 8pt typeface as it spaces the lines such that the connection between them starts to become lost and the eye has to leap from one line to the next.

8pt type on 14pt leading (set +6)

Here – and in the example, shown right – leading opens up the text a bit too much as it looks over spaced.

8pt type on 16pt leading (set +8)

This additional space is distracting when moving the eye from line to line as the gap is uncomfortably large.

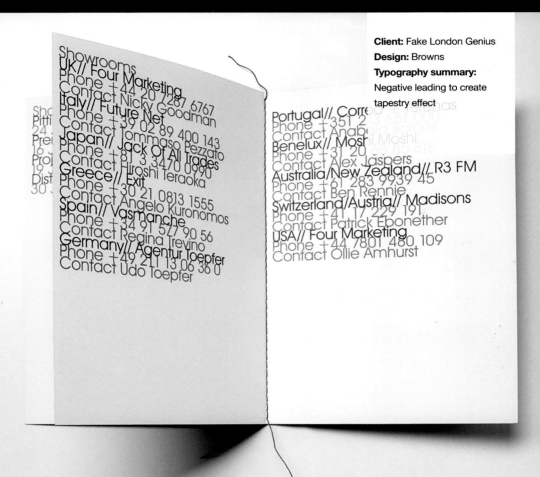

Client: Fake London Genius
Design: Browns
Typography summary: Negative leading to create tapestry effect

Fake London Genius

This Spring / Summer 2005 brochure for Fake London Genius features text that is set with tight, negative leading, resulting in the ascenders butting into the baseline of the line above. This creates a fabric / tapestry effect due to the use of a sans-serif typeface that is alternately coloured in red and black.

Tracking

Tracking refers to the amount of space that exists between letters. This space can be adjusted to make characters more or less distinguishable. Reducing the tracking pares back the space between letters, condenses the text and may allow more text to be fitted into a given area. However, if tracking is reduced too much the letters begin to 'crash' into one another, equally space should not be added to the extent that letters become separated from the words that they are part of.

Normal tracking

This is Garamond Book with normal tracking.

Loose tracking

This is the same typeface set with loose tracking. This is sometimes referred to as letterspacing.

Tight tracking

This is the same typeface set with tight tracking.

Tracking values will affect a whole text block and apply a 'blanket' value to all characters within it. This block is set with a value of -6pt, which creates a block of tightly set text. This is described as being 'darker' as there is a greater proportion of black (type), to white (space).

In contrast a 'lighter' setting is one in which the proportion of white space to black type is increased. This text block is set with a value of +3pt, which creates 'looser' set text, with an airier, 'whiter' overall appearance.

-6pt
When reproduced in a smaller point size, the visual difference becomes more apparent. The more the tracking is reduced, the 'darker' the overall appearance, while a lighter feel is attained using an 'open' tracking value.

0pt
When reproduced in a smaller point size, the visual difference becomes more apparent. The more the tracking is reduced, the 'darker' the overall appearance, while a lighter feel is attained using an 'open' tracking value.

+3pt
When reproduced in a smaller point size, the visual difference becomes more apparent. The more the tracking is reduced, the 'darker' the overall appearance, while a lighter feel is attained using an 'open' tracking value.

When setting text reversed out of black or a colour block you need to add tracking to compensate for the 'creep' of ink.

Thin typefaces can appear 'broken' when reversed, and for this reason heavier weight versions of a typeface are used. The second paragraph here is set in a heavier version of Helvetica Neue.

Kerning

Kerning concerns the space between two letters. Certain letter combinations have too much or too little space between them, which may make some words difficult to read, as you tend to focus on the typographical 'mistakes', as shown below.

This problem can be reduced by kerning, the removal or addition of space between letters. Some letter combinations frequently need to be kerned and are known as kerning pairs. Kerning is used to achieve a balanced look for larger display type, and to handle difficult combinations of letters in body copy.

airport

airport

There are two important rules to remember when kerning text:

1

As type gets bigger you will need to reduce spacing to compensate. The two words above have the same relative kerning values. While the top example looks correctly set, the bottom example is starting to look 'loose' in the middle section and would benefit from being kerned in. The top example has had additional spacing entered between the letters 'r' and 't'.

2

Do not kern type until the tracking values and typeface selections have been set, as the time-consuming fine-adjustments could easily be wasted by any subsequent change. Do not assume that one set of kerning values will transfer to another typeface. Different typefaces possess particular characteristics and so require bespoke kerning – as can be seen opposite.

Akzidenz Grotesk
Even a single word can require a great deal of kerning.

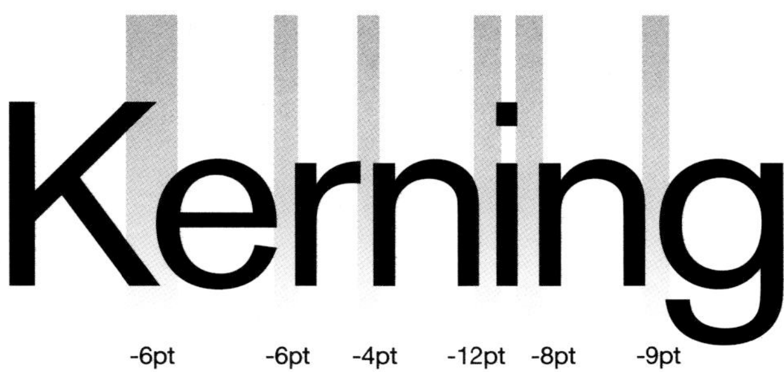

Swiss 721
Here, the same kerning values create uneven distances on either side of the letter 'i'.

Kerning

Benguiat
Here, the same kerning values are collapsing the serifs together.

Kerning

Apollo MT
Here certain pairs are becoming joined, while space is opening between other pairs.

Kerning

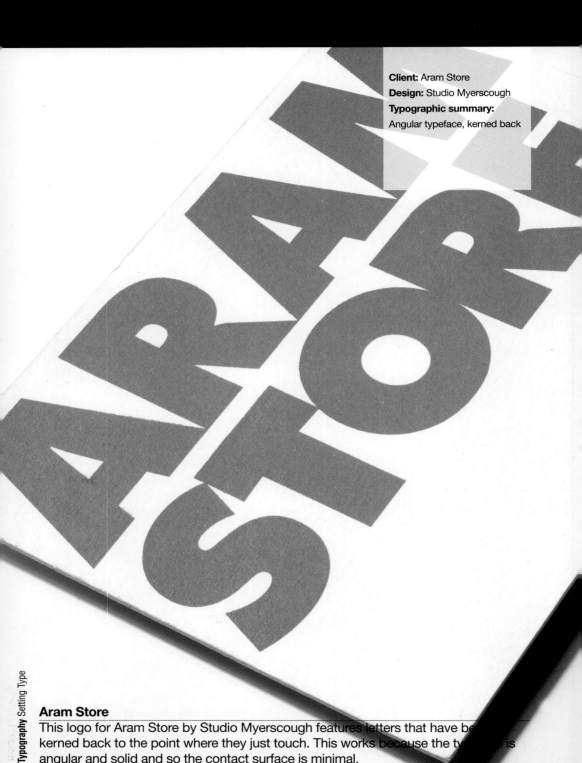

Client: Aram Store
Design: Studio Myerscough
Typographic summary:
Angular typeface, kerned back

Aram Store

This logo for Aram Store by Studio Myerscough features letters that have been kerned back to the point where they just touch. This works because the typeface is angular and solid and so the contact surface is minimal.

Client: Cobella
Design: NB: Studio
Typographic summary: Avant Garde employed as a display type with negative kerning

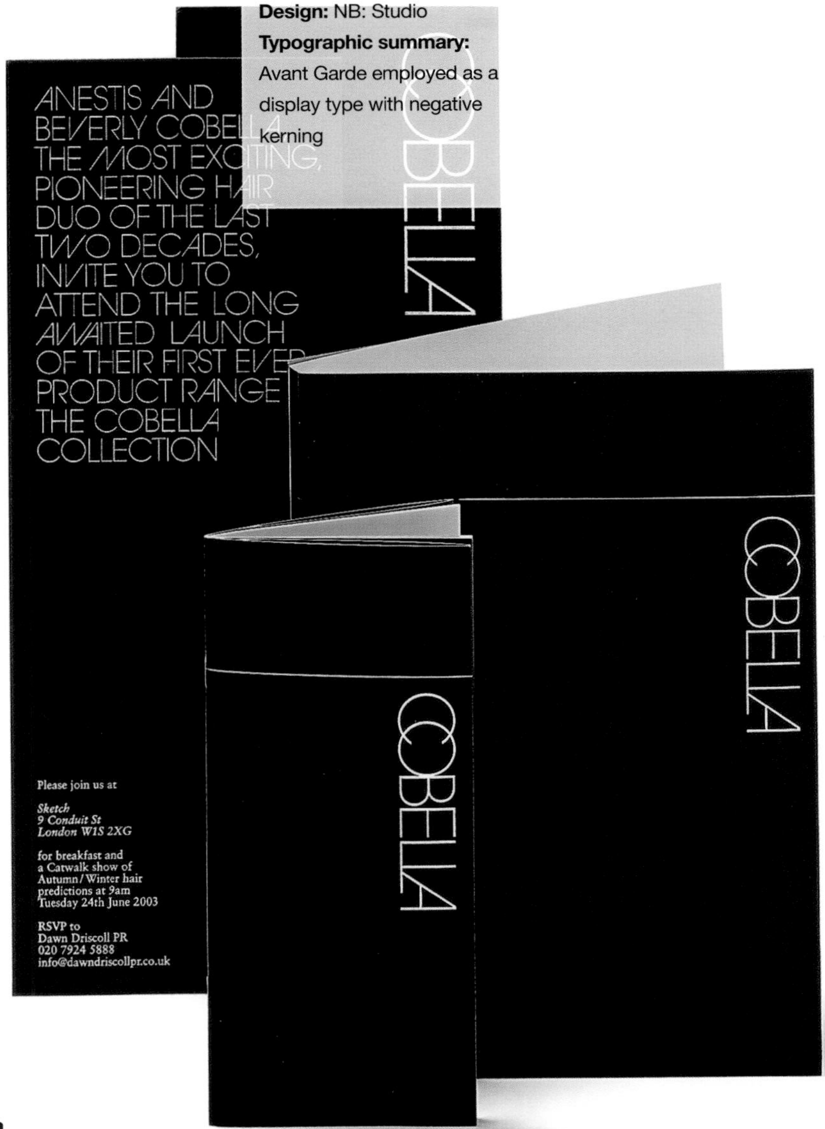

Cobella

To create an identity for a range of hair products by Cobella, NB: Studio used an alternative, display type version of Avant Garde. The standard has upright versions of characters such as 'A', 'M', 'V' and 'W'. The distinctive forward sloping of these characters within this version of the typeface make for individuality but not necessarily legibility. The use of Avant Garde is restricted to a display function and Bell Gothic is used for typesetting additional information. The main logotype is set with negative kerning, which again increases distinction and personality.

Type spacing choices

This is Swiss monospaced type, each character occupies the same width and so it demands more space than other type.

Type spacing choices

This is Swiss proportionally-spaced type, as the letterspacing is proportional to the letter size the text string is more compact and uses less space.

Each of the characters in monospaced typefaces occupy the same width, irrespective of its actual size. These typefaces were originally used on typewriters as they enable the creation of text that aligns in vertical columns to be easily produced. Courier is an example of a monospaced typeface that has become popular in the digital age. Some of the disadvantages of monospaced type are that it has a mechanical appearance, is hard to read and occupies a great deal of space.

Proportionally-spaced type uses a spacing system that was developed by the Monotype and Linotype type foundries, which mimics the letterspacing of historical handset forms. Individual characters occupy a space proportional to their size, this means text takes up less space and is easier to read. However, it is more difficult to align numerals or text vertically if a proportionally-spaced typeface is used.

The use of non-standard capitalisation is increasingly popular in order to create distinguishing points in designs and trademarked terms; for example 'PostScript'. This is referred to as intercaps, bicapitalisation or camel case and is characterised by the joining of compound words or phrases without spacing. Crucially, each term is capitalised. The uneven profile of such words has a supposed resemblance to the two humps of a bactrian camel.

CamelCase

Client: Everything in Between
Design: 3 Deep Design
Typographic summary:
Colliding words, highlighted type

148a Barkly Street
St Kilda Victoria
3182 Australia
T +613 9593 8034
F +613 9534 2414
www.everything.net.au

Everything in between is a series of design workshops, talks and collaborations between students and national and international creative thinkers.

Created by 3 Deep Design.

hellogoodbye
beginningend
monologuedialogue
reactionaction
fictiontruth

everythingbetween™

Brett Phillips
Program Director

hellogoodbye
beginningend
monologuedialogue
reactionaction
fictiontruth

everythingbetween™

hellogoodbye
beginningend
monologuedialogue
reactionaction
fictiontruth

everythingbetween™

With compliments

Trading as 3 Deep Design Pty Ltd
ABN 398 654 330 48

148a Barkly Street
St Kilda Victoria
3182 Australia
T +613 9593 8034
F +613 9534 2414
www.everything.net.au

Everything in between is a series of design workshops, talks and collaborations between students and national and international creative thinkers.

Created by 3 Deep Design.

Everything in Between

This stationery identity, for Everything in Between, by 3 Deep Design features the collision of words – words running into one another without spacing – to provide sound-bite messages such as 'hellogoodbye', 'beginningend', 'fictiontruth' and so on. This approach is also incorporated into the company's logo; 'everythingbetween' as 'in' is highlighted in a different colour.

Overprinting and knocking out

Traditional four-colour printing can be restrictive. Black when printing on its own can often appear pale and unsubstantial. Overprinting can be used to overcome this problem and to add creative layering. To understand overprinting, however, one needs a basic understanding of a process called 'knocking out'.

As the cyan plate overlaps the magenta and yellow plates the type is 'knocked out' (shown above), leaving the three colours intact (i.e. they are solid and not combined or mixed). Shown to the right is a block of solid black ink printed separately, notice the lighter density of the ink colour.

An overprint (or surprint), describes a process where one colour prints directly over the previous colours in the cyan, magenta, yellow and black print order (shown above). When one colour overlaps another both colours print, resulting in a combination of the colours. The black square to the right is printed using all four colours; this is called a four-colour black and has more density than the single print black box above it. This technique of overprinting can be used to add texture to a design.

Metropolis (right)

This newsletter for Metropolis Bookstore uses a series of overprints, primarily the body text overprints the green section headers to add a textural highlight to the columns. By overprinting the darker colour over the lighter, you eliminate mis-registration problems; where slithers of white begin to show if the plates do not marry up correctly.

Client: Metropolis Bookstore

Design: 3 Deep Design

Typographic summary:

Large-point headers overprinted in colour

Fruits
Shoichi Aoki
Phaidon
Coming soon
$55.00 approximately

Fruits is a collection of Tokyo street fashion portraits from Japan's premier street fanzine of the same name. Fruits was established in 1994, by photographer Shoichi Aoki, initially as a project to document the growing explosion in street fashion within the suburbs of Tokyo. Over the past five years, the magazine has grown to cult status and is now avidly followed by thousands of Japanese teenagers who also use the magazine as an opportunity to check out the latest styles and trends. This extensive collections of portraits represents a unique documentation of the changing face of street fashion throughout the last decade. Colourful, fascinating, and funny, this is the first time these cult images have been published outside of Japan. Fruits will delight followers of fashion and youth culture.

Fabric of Fashion
British Council
Coming soon
$50.00 approximately

Fabric of Fashion focuses on the collaboration between the textile and fashion designer, a coalescence that in recent years has emerged as a distinctive characteristic of British Fashion. Published to coincide with an international British Council touring exhibition, the 15 designers included in the exhibition are fashioning garments and accessories from the inside out, questioning the boundaries between two disciplines, challenging assumptions of good design and provoking us to look anew. By asserting the very fabric of their medium, the selected designers seek to re-examine not just the appearance and construction of clothes but other issues too - from environmental and political concerns to highly personal and philosophical ideas. Fabrics, because of the way in which they are produced and the applications for which they are designed, allow these designers freedom to explore a wider range of issues than those offered simply through the conventions of silhouette and style.

Thomas Demand
Francesco Bonami, Regis Durand
Thames and Hudson
Available now
$60.00 approximately

Originally trained as a sculptor, Thomas Demand approaches phot[…] a means of preserving ephemeral paper constructions but inevitab[…] becomes central to his creative process. At first glance, Demand[…] seem to present fragments of a hyperreal and familiar place but, b[…] they reveal their true identity: a wholly artificial world reduced to g[…] For each of his reproductions, Demand constructs life-size models […] and cardboard, and these forms always allow signs of their true n[…] show through.

The Best from Twenty Years of i-D
Terry Jones
Taschen
Coming soon
$100.00 approximately

This heavyweight volume shows every i-D cover and a spread from each of the 204 issues published up to December 2000. In doing so it is as democratic as the aesthetic of the magazine itself. We get the good and the bad, the ugly and the beautiful, the stages of development that have stood the test of time and those that haven't."

Facsimile
Francois Berthoud
Edition Dino Simonett
Coming soon
$70.00 approximately

This publication contains lavish reproductions of magazine pages and artworks by the fashion illustrator Francois Berthoud. His covers, advertisements, freelance work and special features for Interview Magazine amongst numerous others, are brought together for the first time. A must-have for any fashion die-hard. Brightly tinted edgy graphics lead the observer from the punk-inspired spreads of the mid 1980's through to today's neo-classical elegance.

Photographs
Abbas Kiarostami
Hazan
Coming soon
$60.00 approximately

This collection of spellbinding landscape photographs proves that […] Abbas Kiarostami, whose, 'The Taste of Cherry' (Le Gout de la Ce[…] Palme d'Or at Cannes in 1997, should be similarly commended fo[…] photography. Taken in Kurdistan and northern Iran during location shooting for his latest film, 'Ceremonie Speciale', the images here present us with the same mystical universe, the same clarity, and the same sense of symbol and allegory as Kiarostami's cinematic work. At the same time however, we are struck by one major difference between his films and the photographs contained here: except for a single solitary dog, humans and animals are absent from these photographs – it is though one of Kiarostami's films had been frozen, and all of its narrative structures and interpersonal relationships erased, leaving only these sublime and mysterious tableaux. This sumptuously designed book also contains an introductory interview with the filmmaker, conducted by noted French scholar, Michel Ciment.

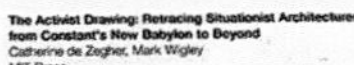

Objects to Use
Gijs Bakker
010
Coming Soon
$75.00 approximately

Gijs Bakker belongs to a select group of Dutch designers who have risen to international importance. His work is regarded as exemplary of the waywardness of Dutch design: modernistic and minimal at times combined with an absurd sense of humour. Well known for his jewelry, Bakker's industrial, interior and exhibition stand designs have been less conspicuous, as has his founding role in Droog Design. His chairs, temporary buildings, restaurant interiors, lamps, candle holders, bike racks, and pens are documented here, with a commentary essay by Ida van Zijl. The book comes wrapped in an innovative dust jacket.

Inside Cars
J. Abbott Miller
Princeton Architectural Press
Coming soon
$40.00 approximately

Inside Cars examines this unusual space through a range of media, including photography, video, sculpture, and painting. Alex Harris photographs windshields and dashboards of 50 year old cars in Havana; Nan Goldin's intensely personal photographs reveal the emotions played out inside this intimate space; Greil Marcus considers music as a component of the car; Phil Patton images the design of car interiors of the future; Paul Arthur traces the shifting image of the car as expressed in film noir. This book is the first in a series that marks the transformation of the award-winning 2wice magazine into hardcover book format.

Industrial Design
Jasper Morrison
Lars Muller
Coming soon
$200.00 approximately

This publication provides a long-needed survey of the working methods and results achieved by one of the most influential European product designers. His is an approach that many designers return to: simple and durable form, functional and true to its materials. Morrison has developed an unmistakable and excitingly modern formal language that is used by manufacturers including FSB, Vitra, Cappellini and Flos.

Integral Ruedi Baur et Associes
Lars Muller
Coming Soon
$120.00 approximately

Integral Ruedi Baur is one of Europe's leading design studios. This publication brings together the most remarkable results from the past few years including corporate design programmes and scenographic interventions for a number of European museums, including the renovated Centre Pompidou. Here graphic design's extension into architecture becomes increasingly apparent.

Zines
Booth-Clibborn
Coming Soon
$90.00 approximately

With over 400 illustrations, this book showcases a large range of international current zines, put into context by historical examples from the hoardings of a number of die-hard collectors.

Malaparte: A House Like Me
Michael McDonough
Clarkson N. Potter
Available now
$120.00 approximately

Casa Malaparte is the famous house in which Godard's 'Le Mepris' was filmed. With a foreword by Tom Wolfe, Malaparte: A House Like Me is organised and edited by noted architect, designer, and writer Michael McDonough, and brings together the combined efforts of artists, historians, architects, and writers to unlock the meanings and mysteries behind Casa Malaparte. Provocative essays, sketches, and speculative projects by, among others, Philip Locale, Robert Venturi, Carla Fendi, Karl Lagerfeld, Willem Dafoe, Grant Morrison, Coleman Andrews and Philippe Starck explore the imagery, poetics, and social significance of Casa Malaparte. Also included are two dozen stunning photographs of the house taken by renowned photographer Mimmo Jodice.

3D-2D/Designers Republic
Ole Bouman, Jeffrey Kipnis
Laurence King
$120.00 approximately

Created by the people at The Designers Republic, one of today's most revered design firms, 3D-2D/Designers Republic explores new ways of communicating architecture. By recreating a three-dimensional building in the form of a printed publication, this innovative book attempts to expand and open up new approaches to presenting and experiencing architectural products, based on the firm's own products and research from over the past ten years.

The book takes as its subject the CCIS Office Building (Chamber of Commerce and Industry of Slovenia) which was designed by Sadar + Vuga, an up-and-coming architectural practice. Both provocative and interactive, this unique case study reinvents the architectural drawing in ways that force the reader to rethink his relationship to buildings, to drawings, and to space in general. As visionary as it is fun to read, 3D-2D is a user-friendly book in a post electronic, post CD-ROM, post-DVD era -- one that challenges the potentials of a book as a medium in itself.

The Activist Drawing: Retracing Situationist Architectures from Constant's New Babylon to Beyond
Catherine de Zegher, Mark Wigley
MIT Press
Coming soon
$70.00 approximately

Working before the current debate about architecture in the supposedly placeless electronic age, Constant conceived an urban and architectural model that literally envisaged the World Wide Web. The inhabitants of his New Babylon drift through huge labyrinthine interiors, perpetually reconstructing every aspect of the environment according to their latest desires. Walls, floors, lighting, sound, colour, texture, and smell keep changing. This network of vast "sectors" can be seen as a physical embodiment of the Internet, where people configure their individual Web sites and wander from site to site without limits. With its parallels to our virtual world, New Babylon seems as radical today as when it was created.

Colours: Rem Koolhaas/OMA, Norman Foster, Alessandro Mendini
Birkhauser
Coming soon
$30.00 approximately

"The nature of colour should change – no longer just a thin layer of change, but something that genuinely alters perception" – this stipulation of Rem Koolhaas is echoed by the world famous architects and designers Alessandro Mendini and Norman Foster. In this volume they present between them a total of 90 colours – each covering half a page – accompanied by comments on the background, the significance and the application of the colours.

Architecture Goes Wild – Manifest Writings
Kas Oosterhuis
010
Coming soon
$100.00 approximately

Kas Oosterhuis bridges the gap between theory and practice considering science fiction in architectural practice. Viewing the future of architecture, he proposes the concept of adapting buildings, which think in real time and move following a pattern of behaviour. Accompanied with lavish illustrations of Oosterhuis's projects.

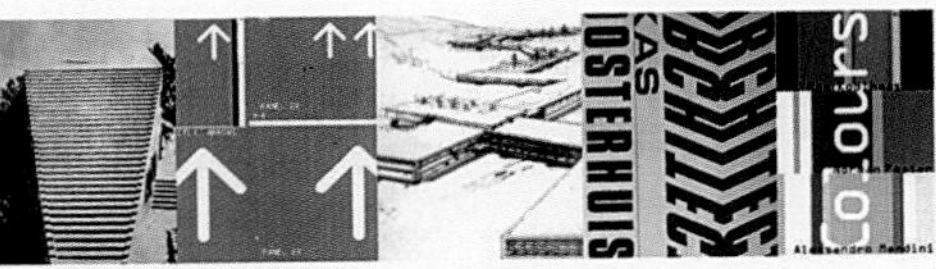

Extreme Canvas: Movie Poster Paintings from Ghana
Ernie Wolfe III
Dilettante Press
Available now
$100.00 approximately

In the 1980s a group of entrepreneurs in Ghana created small-scale, mobile film-distribution empires, hitting the road with videocassettes, television monitors, portable gas-powered generators and rolled-up, hand-painted, artist signed canvas posters. This new medium created the first opportunity for some of the best young painters in Ghana to express themselves on a public scale. In the frequent absence of an original image upon which to base the work they had been commissioned to produce, the artists inevitably created cinematic paintings that were largely interpretive and imagination-driven. In the book's four major essays, author Ernie Wolfe III recounts the rise and fall of the mobile cinema tradition, while noted African art scholar Roy Sieber follows two-dimensional art in Africa from rock paintings in the Sahara to contemporary manuals, wall paintings, and barber board paintings as well as the canvas movie posters themselves; Paul Hayes Tucker compares the phenomenon to 19th century European utility based painting; and poet and art critic John Yau contributes the perspective of an American art historian. In addition, Hollywood film notables such as horror auteur Clive Barker, actor LeVar Burton, actress Anjelica Huston, and director Gus Van Sant contribute chapter introductions.

It Crossed My Mind
Marijke Van Warmerdam
Oktagon
Available now
$75.00 approximately

The film and video work of Marijke van Warmerdam occupies a hybrid position somewhere between film, installation, photography and sculpture. Her large scale projections are almost all made on film, but they are not films. They are loops, shown in the lit white space of the gallery; but they are not installations since they do not enclose or engage physical space. The film images have a richness of colour, texture and surface which allies them more with photography than with the diffused electronic surface of video. Yet the images are not photographic. Van Warmerdam's apparently simple forms defy definition precisely because they operate in an ambiguous space within which the distinctions between one formal structure and another, and between artifice and reality are deliberately blurred.

Metropolis Studio Application Form

Name
Address
Telephone
Email
Profession
I am a current reading lounge member Y☐ N☐
I have read and understand the terms of Metropolis Studio
Signature
Date

APPLICATION FORM

Metropolis is a reward system for art and design professionals. As a member you will receive the following advantages:

• A gift voucher to the value of 10% of purchases made during the 6 month period • Invitations to sales previews and special events • Use of the reward system at our other stores, Cosmos and Antipodes.

The conditions of use include: • It is applicable to book purchases only • It cannot be used on sale or discounted items • It cannot be used for on-line purchases • With the exception of the initial 6 month period, $300 must be spent to receive the gift voucher • Metropolis reserves the right to alter conditions of the scheme.

Senses of Cinema
www.sensesofcinema.com

An online film journal devoted to the serious and eclectic discussion of cinema. Adrian Martin (The Age) "Australia,s best movie journal".

Paintings, Photographs, Films
Dennis Hopper
Stedelijk Museum
Coming soon
$80.00 approximately

Dennis Hopper is best known for his films, as an actor and director, and for his Bohemian lifestyle. This publication focuses on his paintings, which are linked to Hopper's photographs, and to a certain extent, to his movies. He uses photographs and film stills in his canvases, and often puts together several works into diptychs and other multiple combinations. This publication demonstrates the multifaceted nature of Hopper the artist and the ambiguity and changeability of his image – from cult figure to introvert painter. The book includes an essay by Rudi Fuchs an an article by Jan-Hein Sassen.

Hitchcock and Art – Fatal Coincidences
Mazzotta Edizione
Coming Soon
$100.00 approximately

Devoting an exhibition to a filmmaker – let alone possibly the most famous of all filmmakers – is a daunting but legitimate challenge. Philosophers, art historians and contemporary artists have all found new inspirations for their own works within a body of cinematic work whose apparent emphasis on spectacle no longer appears at odds with its borrowings from learned, literary and pictorial culture. The films of Hitchcock command attention because they stemmed from a broader view of cinema that encompasses other art forms as well as the mysteries of the human psyche. The Hitchcockian oeuvre of Romantic constancy, Symbolist style and Surrealist influence are explored in this intelligent, well written overview of a prolific genius that has had a profound effect on our culture.

Legibility and readability

These two terms are often used synonymously, however, legibility refers to the ability to distinguish one letterform from another via the physical characteristics that are inherent in the design of a particular typeface, such as x-height, character shapes, counter size, stroke contrast, and type weight. The legibility of a piece of body text is enforced by the use of standard point sizes, sensitive leading and appropriate alignment. Absolute clarity of information combined with a minimum of interfering factors creates legible type.

Readability concerns the properties of a piece of type or design that affect the ability to 'understand' it. For example, the spreads opposite have reduced legibility, but the text conveys a dynamic sense of movement, which shapes our opinions about the information the design contains.

Client: Who's Next
Design: Research Studios
Typographic summary: Sans-serif type used as graphic device with intentionally reduced readability

Who's Next

This corporate identity was designed by Research Studios for Who's Next, which is a top international fashion event held in France. The commercial guide pictured features disjointed typography, which is used as a graphical device so that the letters of a word do not track in an expected manner, and results in diminished readability. The use of different type sizes and weights further compounds this. As the text is used as a graphical device, readability of the complete text string takes secondary importance to the individual words.

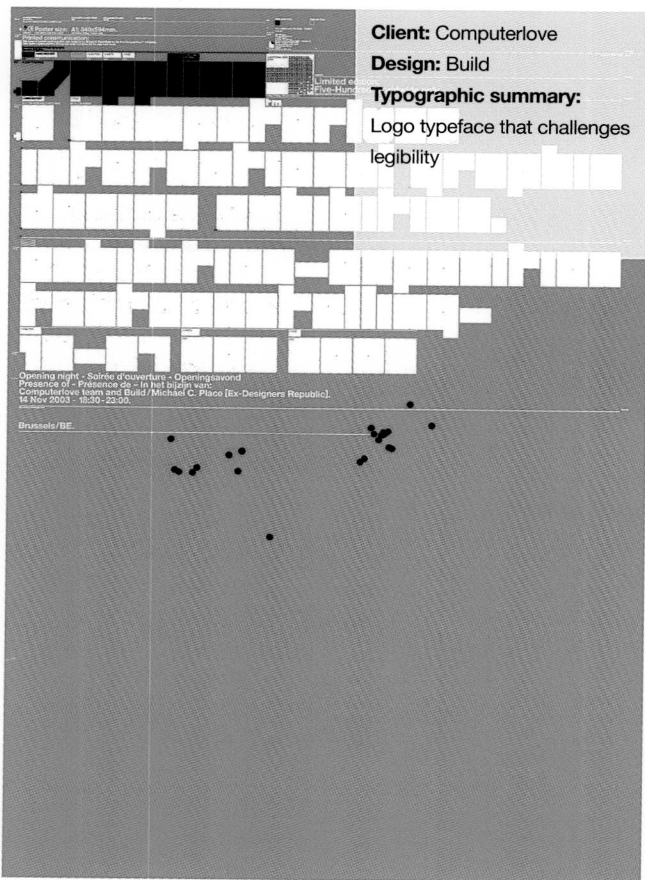

Client: Computerlove

Design: Build

Typographic summary: Logo typeface that challenges legibility

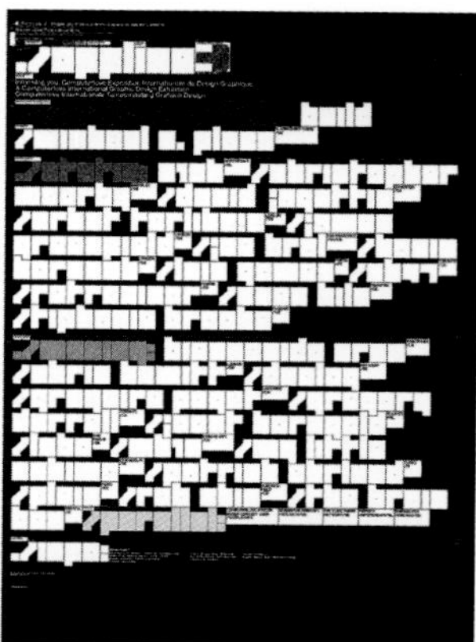

Build

This poster, pictured front and back and designed by Build for Computerlove, provides a wonderful example of type characteristics affecting legibility. The letterforms and absence of counters makes the text very difficult to read, which is somewhat incongruous as posters are primarily used as a medium to inform. This diminished legibility creates a strong visual impact that is perhaps more important than any information that the reader would receive from the text. Essentially, the design informs the viewer just as much as deciphering the text would.

Cognitive meaning

The cognitive meaning of an object or image is what we have learned to know or understand from looking at it. For example, we have learned that red is associated with danger and that '?' means a question has been asked or posed. Graphic designers use cognitive aspects in their designs to produce desired reactions from the reader or viewer.

Denotative meaning

Images are frequently used for their denotative meanings because they explicitly denote or designate something. For example, from an image of musical instruments we assume that the subject has something to do with music. The inherent ability of an image to denote or suggest something is a key part of the graphic design process.

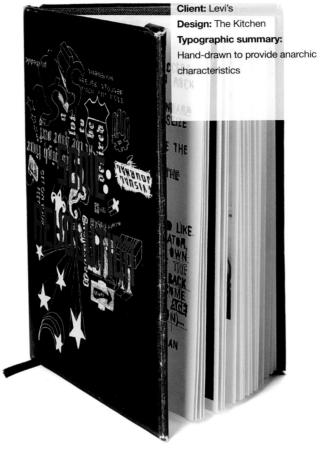

Client: Levi's

Design: The Kitchen

Typographic summary:

Hand-drawn to provide anarchic characteristics

Levi's

This brochure, for clothing manufacturer Levi's and designed by The Kitchen, uses 'Sonic Revolution' as the central theme of the clothing styles it displays.

The design features aggressive, anarchic and immediate hand-drawn type to convey these qualities and associate them with the clothing brand. The design also mimics the diary or journal of a teenager, enforcing the appeal to the target market for the clothing.

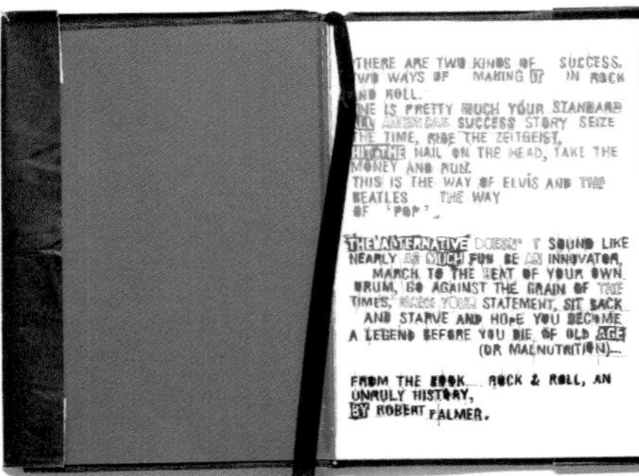

Fiction
New Work by BalletLab

Venue
Chunky Move
111 Sturt Street
Southbank VIC
Reservations
CUB Malthouse
9685 5111
Tickets
$20 Full
$15 Concession

Dates
Thursday 19th – Saturday
21st August at 8.30pm
Tuesday 24th – Saturday
28th August at 8.30pm
Sunday 29th August at 5pm
Post show forum Tuesday
24th August

Choreography
Phillip Adams and
Rebecca Hilton
Live sound composition
Lynton Carr
Performers
Brooke Stamp, Ryan Lowe
Carlee Mellow, Joanne
White, Tim Harvey,
Clair Peters and Edgar
John Wegner

Lighting
Ben Cisterne
Costumes
Graham Green
Graphic Design
3 Deep Design
Photography
Jeff Busby

Proudly sponsored by

Client: Balletlab

Design: 3 Deep Design

Typographic summary:

Typeface generated from background pattern

Type Generation

Type generation refers to the different applications or approaches used to create letterforms. This can be as part of a deliberate and involved process undertaken to design a new typeface, or as simple as spray-painting the letters required. The unifying theme in this section is that typography may be manipulated in many different ways and taken from many different sources in order to serve specific design purposes. In this way, designers harness attributes in the generated type in order to add to, or reinforce, the message they want to convey via the design.

Bespoke type generation, whilst potentially time consuming, undoubtedly results in something unique and personal. This is often what an organisation is seeking when it commissions a design studio to create a new identity on its behalf. The adaptation of existing typefaces can also produce results suitable for this end without having to reinvent the wheel.

The examples within this chapter demonstrate some of the many ways of approaching type generation. Whether using exacting and complex grid formations – as the example opposite demonstrates – or returning to more basic mark-making techniques, type generation offers many more possibilities than existing, well-distributed typefaces. Although many of these examples are experimental, the basic principles discussed previously remain valid. The generation and setting of these typefaces isn't accidental – they are produced within the larger context of typographical conventions, even if they push the boundaries.

Balletlab (left)

Created for Balletlab by 3 Deep Design, this poster uses a typeface that was developed from the background pattern. The pattern limits the character shapes that can be produced and provides an inclined baseline for the text. The result is text that is dynamic, contemporary and evocative of the subject matter it conveys.

Font generation

Although there are thousands of different typefaces available sometimes, it may still be necessary to create a new one. Fonts can be produced in a number of different ways; from creating original art to replicating type from older publications, or from mark making to rendering type in a dedicated font-generation program. The motivation for undertaking this effort is usually the desire to create a unique, bespoke, typographical solution for a project. The examples shown here have been constructed, built, rendered and created for specific design applications. Many of these examples not only result in engaging designs, but also challenge the very fabric of what we may feel constitutes a typeface.

Fringe Fashion (right)

This poster, for the Fringe Fashion festival created by 3 Deep Design, uses a typeface that has stems that incorporate overtly exaggerated diagonals. This can be seen with the letters 'F' and 'R' as the characters appear as if they are bending forward rather than having a straight stem, which is more common.

Client: Fringe Fashion
Design: 3 Deep Design
Typographic summary:
Font that incorporates exaggerated diagonal stems

FRINGE FASHION
presented by Melbourne Fringe and Melbourne Metro Nightclub
10 May 2000

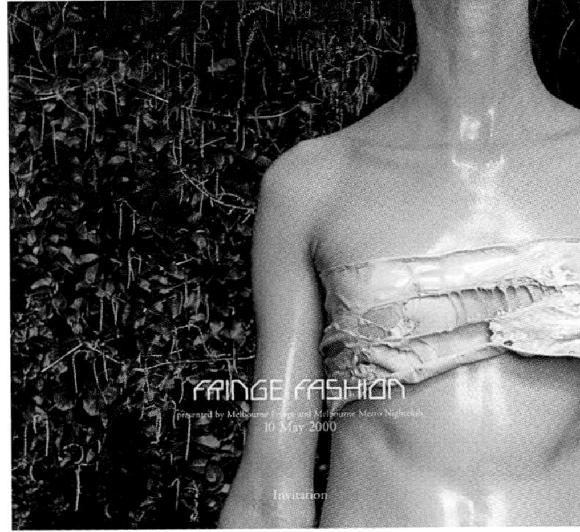

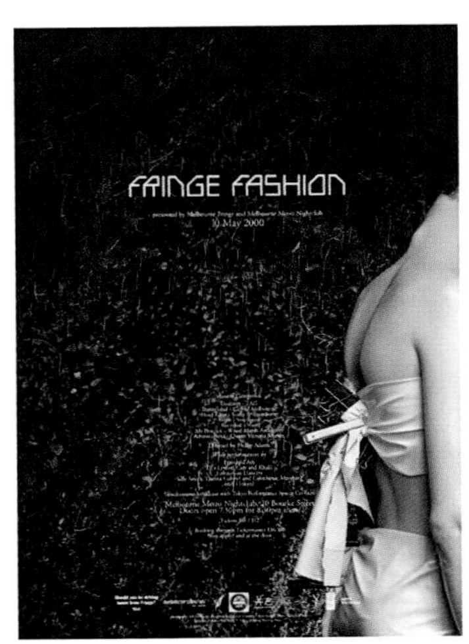

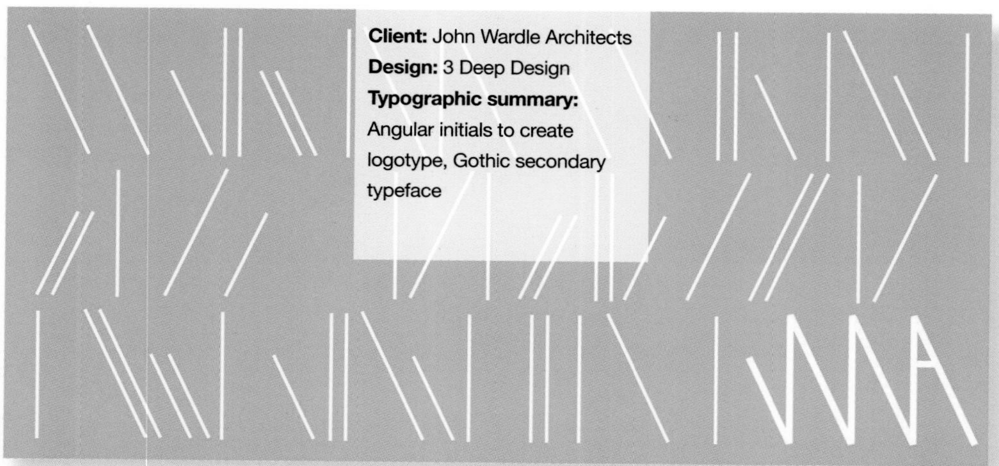

Client: John Wardle Architects
Design: 3 Deep Design
Typographic summary:
Angular initials to create logotype, Gothic secondary typeface

John Wardle
B Arch FRAIA M.Arch
Principal

John Wardle Architects
Level 10
180 Russell Street
Melbourne Victoria
3000 Australia

Telephone
+61 3 9654 8700
Facsimile
+61 3 9654 8755
Email
johnwardle@
johnwardlearchitects.com

John Wardle Architects (above)

This identity for John Wardle Architects, by 3 Deep Design, presents the initials 'J', 'W' and 'A' in an extremely angular fashion. The acute angles created are repeated as random elements throughout the design, and are only combined together as a whole in its inner pages. The abstract typeface is used as a graphic device and presents a unique visual identity. This contrasts with the Gothic secondary typeface, which is selected for legibility.

Whitechapel Gallery (right)

This bespoke typeface provides both a high degree of individuality and instant recognition for London's Whitechapel Gallery. A consistent and considered application across all media – the example shown here is an events brochure – maintains and fosters association and recognition. The pattern-rich typeface is restricted to the logotype, and a secondary, slab-serif typeface, adds clarity and gravity.

Client: Whitechapel Gallery
Design: Spin
Typographic summary: Bespoke, intricate typeface that provides individuality

June — August 2003
Issue 06
£1

Janet Cardiff &
George Bures Miller -
Recent works

Philip-lorca di Corcia -
A Storybook Life

Events listings,
East London feature
Preview-
Franz West

Whitechapel

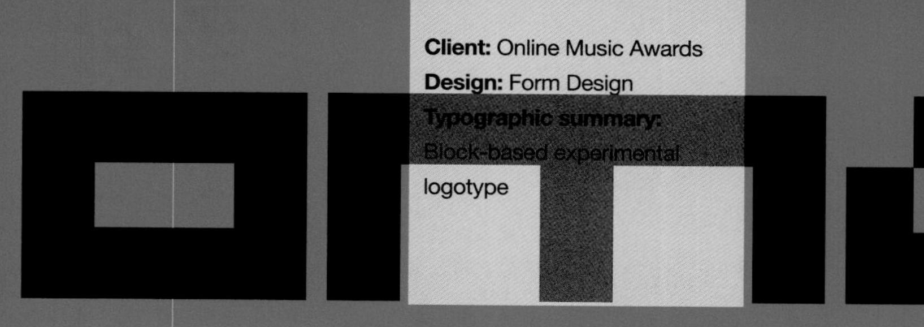

Client: Online Music Awards

Design: Form Design

Typographic summary: Block-based experimental logotype

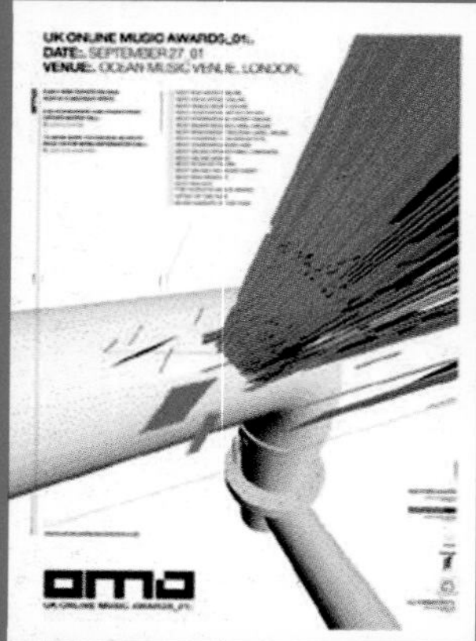

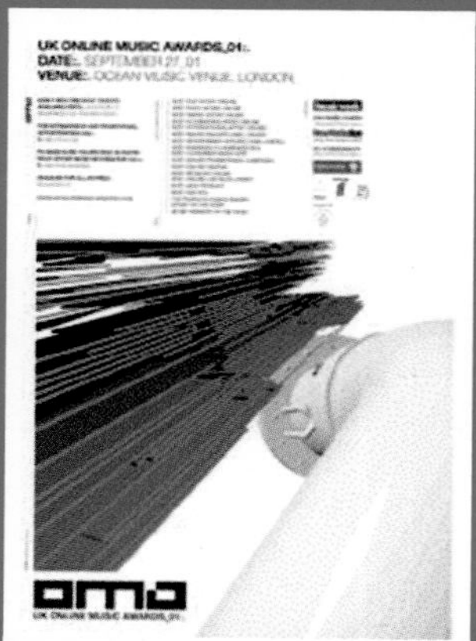

Online Music Awards (above)

These posters were created by Form Design and used to promote the Online Music Awards. They feature a logotype whose characters are generated from blocks. The difference between the ‘a’ and the ‘o’ is, quite simply, the removal of one of these blocks. This rigid use of a small configuration grid results in a bold and angular logotype that is complemented by the use of two different weights of Helvetica.

Made in Clerkenwell (right)

This typeface, created by Research Studios, was designed to promote ‘Made in Clerkenwell’, an open event held in central London. To reflect the precise and crafted artisanal nature of the works exhibited (including ceramics, textiles and jewellery), a hand-drawn type was developed.

The typeface was generated using vector paths, as these can be quickly manipulated to obtain the desired shape and style for each letter. Each character is created using lines of the same width, ensuring consistency and a degree of uniformity from letter to letter.

Client: Clerkenwell Studios
Design: Research Studios
Typographic summary:
Hand-drawn type created through the use of vector paths

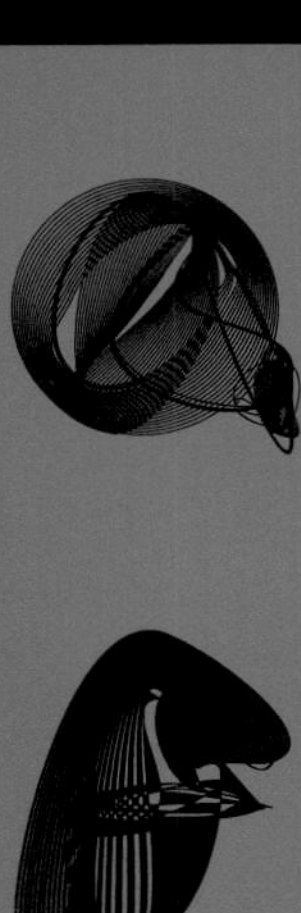

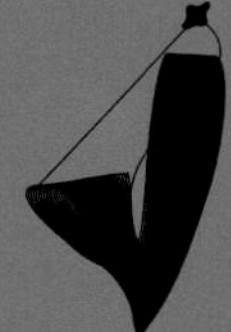

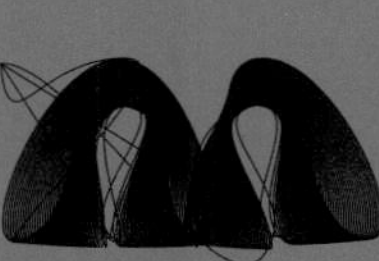

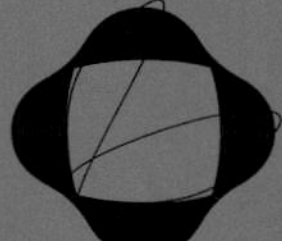

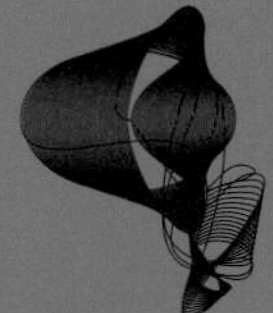

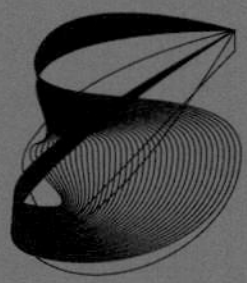

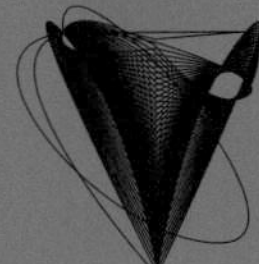

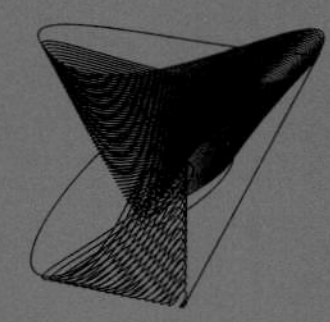

Hand-drawn type

Although there have been many attempts to emulate handwriting in type, none compare to those inherent idiosyncrasies – generated from changes in pressure, speed and concentration – that grace handwritten script. The only way to obtain the unpolished feel of handwritten script is to draw the typography and return to mark making in its most basic form. For some this is a reaction against the occasionally bland nature of modernist typography.

abcdefghijklmnopqrstuvwxyz

Pepita

Designed in 1959 by Imre Reiner, Pepita simulates the spontaneous strokes of the handwritten word.

abcdefghijklmnopqrstuvwxyz

Biffo

David Marshall created Biffo in 1964, this typeface emulates the strokes of a broad-tipped pen. This can be seen in its round and flexible figures and vertical strokes, which have rounded edges to soften the characters. Biffo is suitable for short and mid-length blocks of texts as well as headlines.

abcdefghijklmnopqrstuvwxyz

Snell Roundhand

Snell Roundhand was designed in 1965 by Matthew Carter and is based on 18th century round-hand scripts. It has an elegant and festive feel that is suited to mid-length blocks of text and headlines.

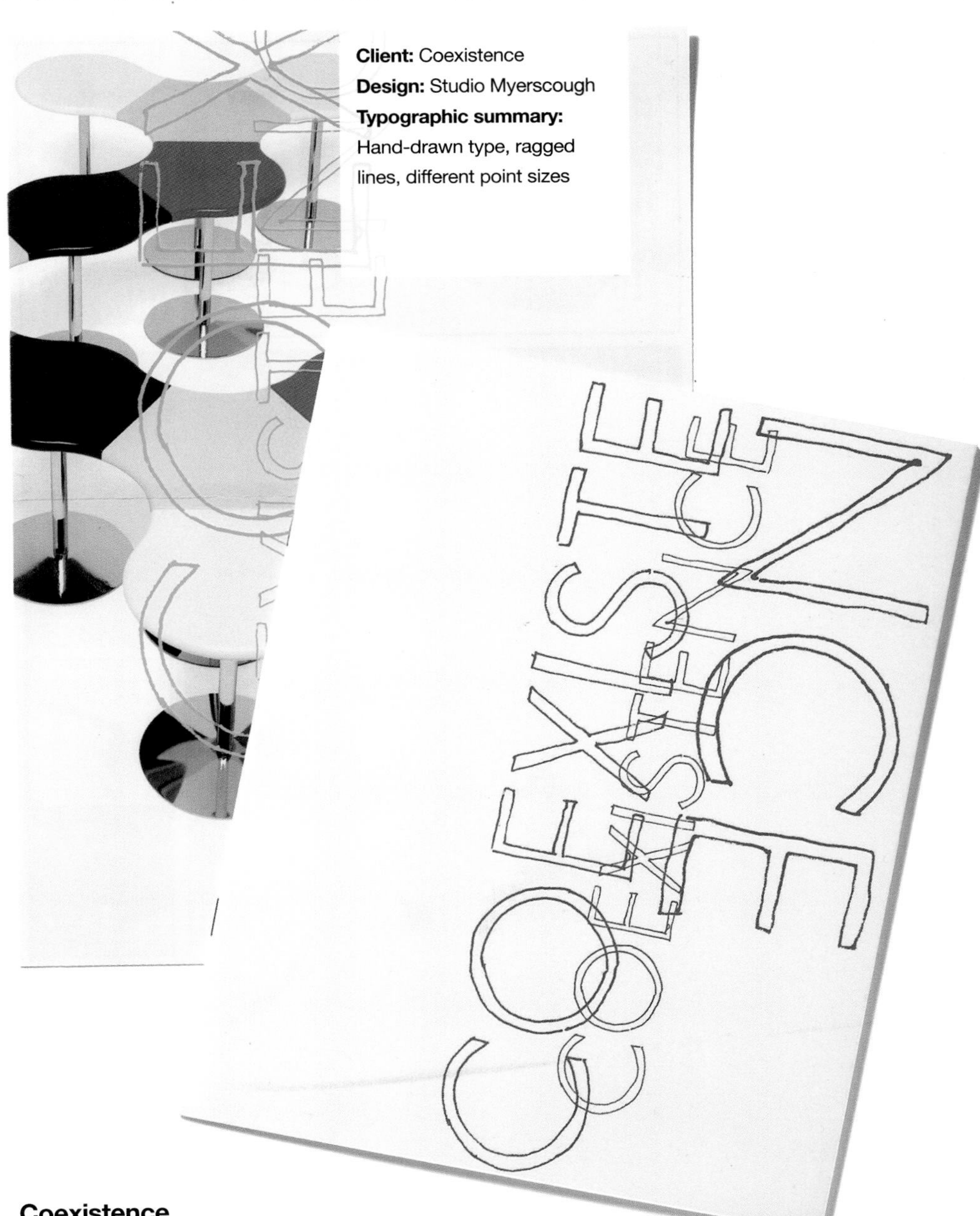

Client: Coexistence
Design: Studio Myerscough
Typographic summary: Hand-drawn type, ragged lines, different point sizes

Coexistence

To create the identity for furniture company Coexistence, Studio Myerscough used a hand-drawn typeface with intentionally rough edges. The characters were typeset in different point sizes and overlapped one another. The almost brutal handling of the typography makes a strong counterpoint to the refined lines of the furniture, and the immediacy of the typography also conveys a playful sense of 'sketch', reminding us of the designed and bespoke nature of the product.

Client: Salvation Army
Design: Browns
Typographic summary: Letterforms constructed from neon tubes

Salvation Army

To create a logo and identity for the youth section of the Salvation Army, design studio Browns created a neon sign to display the slogan A LOVE+. The studio used the outline of the tubes that comprised the neon sign (above), to build the letterforms of the logotype (below). The logotype includes representations of the notches, gaps, bends and blanked-out sections of the glass tubes in the neon sign. These features were then painted out in the logotype.

Client: Jeff Busby
Design: 3 Deep Design
Typographic summary:
Letterforms built on to a geometric grid

Jeff Busby

This identity, for photographer Jeff Busby, by 3 Deep Design uses a strong geometric grid from which the letterforms are built. This restricts the shape of the characters but results in something unique for the client.

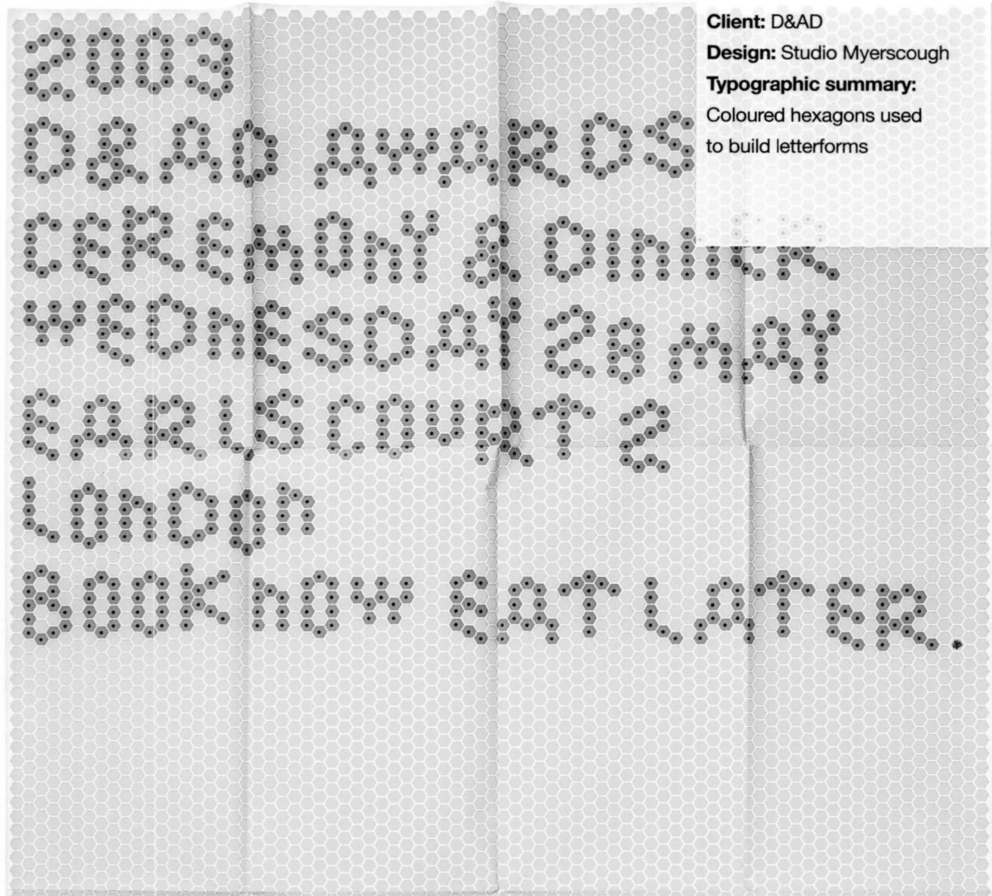

Client: D&AD
Design: Studio Myerscough
Typographic summary:
Coloured hexagons used to build letterforms

D&AD (above)

This invitation and poster for D&AD by Studio Myerscough uses a hexagonal pattern to create the letterforms. The result is a perspective that resembles looking down on to a large box of yellow pencils into which some blue ones are randomly dispersed.

University of Portsmouth (right)

Design studio Radley Yeldar created this prospectus – in the form of an ideas book – for the University of Portsmouth's design courses. The scrapbook-style publication contained all the information prospective students required in order to make a decision about the institution, and also included blank pages at the end to encourage them to begin to explore their own creativity. Much of the information was handwritten in a variety styles. The rawness of the mark making, the hand-drawn letterforms and assorted sketches lends the publication authenticity. The typography is made integral to the publication and is 'rendered' rather than typeset.

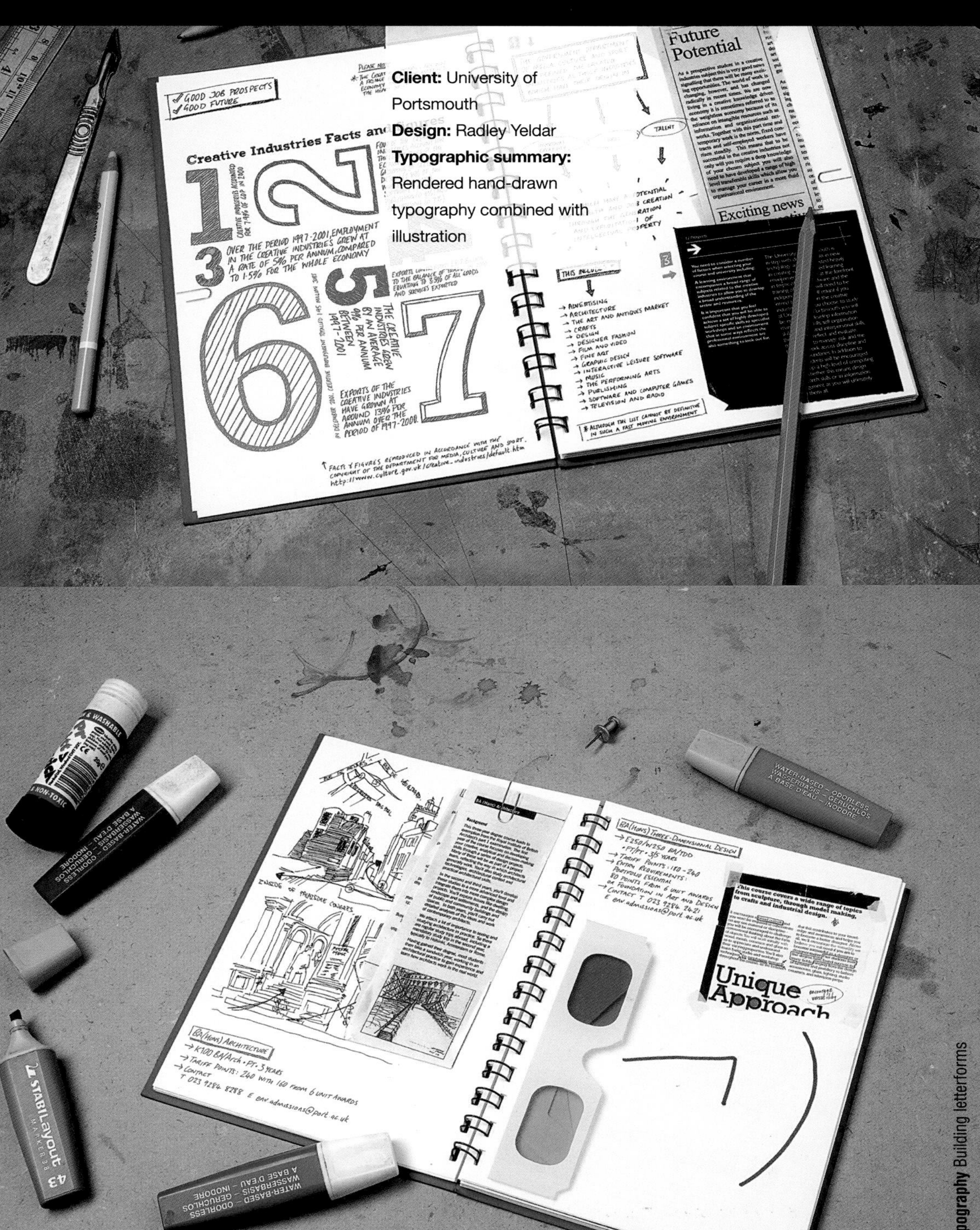

Client: University of Portsmouth
Design: Radley Yeldar
Typographic summary: Rendered hand-drawn typography combined with illustration

Client: Victionary

Design: Build

Typographic summary:
Blocky appearance of characters due to absence of counters and low ascender height

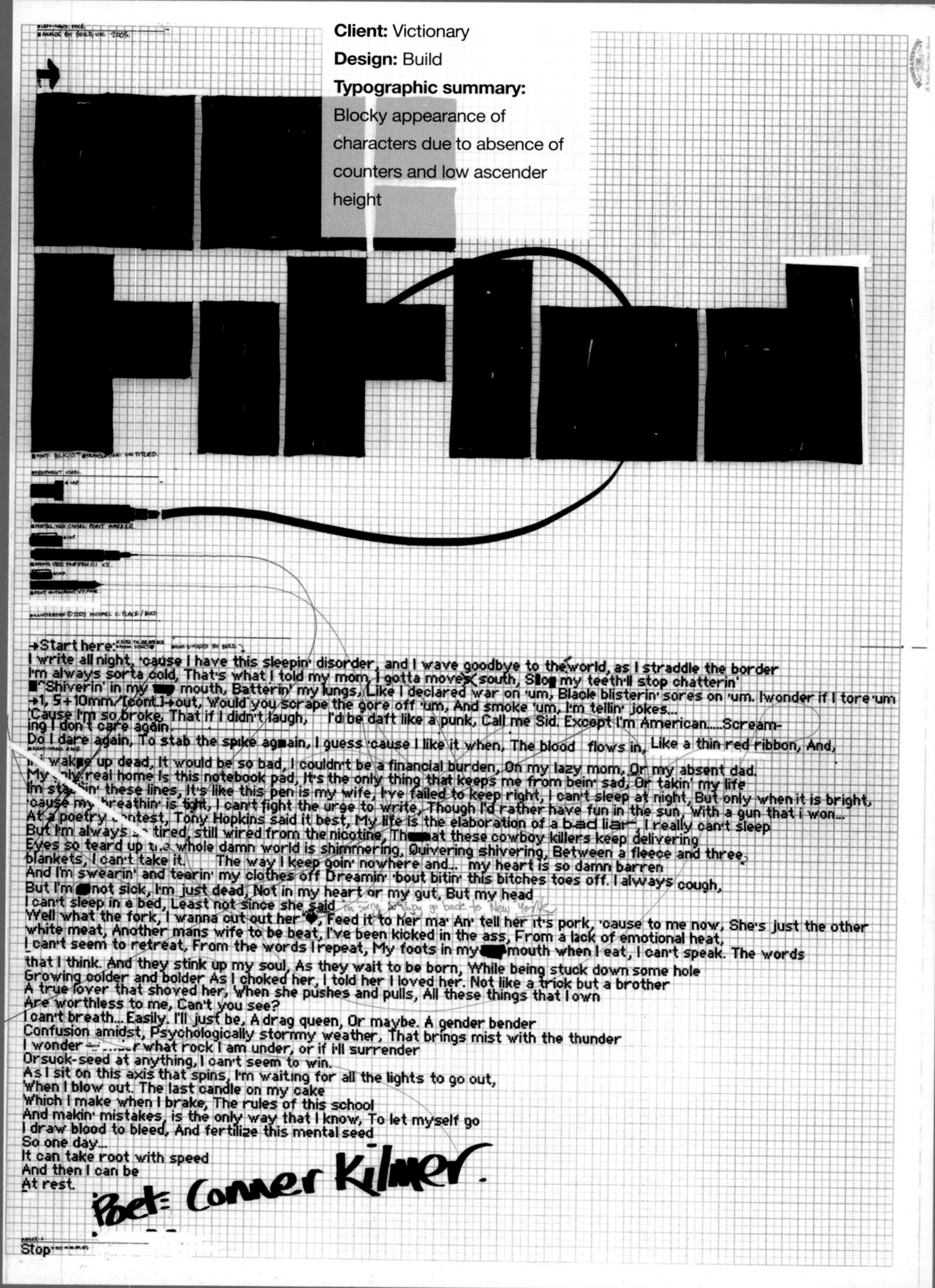

→Start here:
I write all night, 'cause I have this sleepin' disorder, and I wave goodbye to the world, as I straddle the border
I'm always sorta cold, That's what I told my mom, I gotta move south, So my teeth'll stop chatterin'
"Shiverin' in my mouth, Batterin' my lungs, Like I declared war on 'um, Black blisterin' sores on 'um. I wonder if I tore 'um
→1, 5+10mm/[cont.]→out, Would you scrape the gore off 'um, And smoke 'um, I'm tellin' jokes...
'Cause I'm so broke, That if I didn't laugh, I'd be daft like a punk, Call me Sid. Except I'm American.....Scream-
ing I don't care again.
Do I dare again, To stab the spike again, I guess 'cause I like it when, The blood flows in, Like a thin red ribbon, And,
if I wake up dead, It would be so bad, I couldn't be a financial burden, On my lazy mom, Or my absent dad.
My only real home is this notebook pad, It's the only thing that keeps me from bein' sad, Or takin' my life
I'm stackin' these lines, It's like this pen is my wife, I've failed to keep right, I can't sleep at night, But only when it is bright,
'cause my breathin' is tight, I can't fight the urge to write, Though I'd rather have fun in the sun, With a gun that i won...
At a poetry contest, Tony Hopkins said it best, My life is the elaboration of a bad liar, I really can't sleep
But I'm always so tired, still wired from the nicotine, That these cowboy killers keep delivering
Eyes so teard up the whole damn world is shimmering, Quivering shivering, Between a fleece and three
blankets, I can't take it. The way I keep goin' nowhere and... my heart is so damn barren
And I'm swearin' and tearin' my clothes off Dreamin' 'bout bitin' this bitches toes off. I always cough,
But I'm not sick, I'm just dead, Not in my heart or my gut, But my head
I can't sleep in a bed, Least not since she said
Well what the fork, I wanna cut out her ♥, Feed it to her ma' An' tell her it's pork, 'cause to me now, She's just the other
white meat, Another mans wife to be beat, I've been kicked in the ass, From a lack of emotional heat,
I can't seem to retreat, From the words I repeat, My foots in my mouth when I eat, I can't speak. The words
that I think. And they stink up my soul, As they wait to be born, While being stuck down some hole
Growing colder and bolder As I choked her, I told her I loved her. Not like a trick but a brother
A true lover that shoved her, When she pushes and pulls, All these things that I own
Are worthless to me, Can't you see?
I can't breath... Easily. I'll just be, A drag queen, Or maybe. A gender bender
Confusion amidst, Psychologically stormy weather, That brings mist with the thunder
I wonder what rock I am under, or if i'll surrender
Or suck-seed at anything, I can't seem to win.
As I sit on this axis that spins, I'm waiting for all the lights to go out,
When I blow out. The last candle on my cake
Which I make when I brake, The rules of this school
And makin' mistakes, is the only way that I know, To let myself go
I draw blood to bleed, And fertilize this mental seed
So one day...
It can take root with speed
And then I can be
At rest.

Poet: Conner Kilmer.

Stop

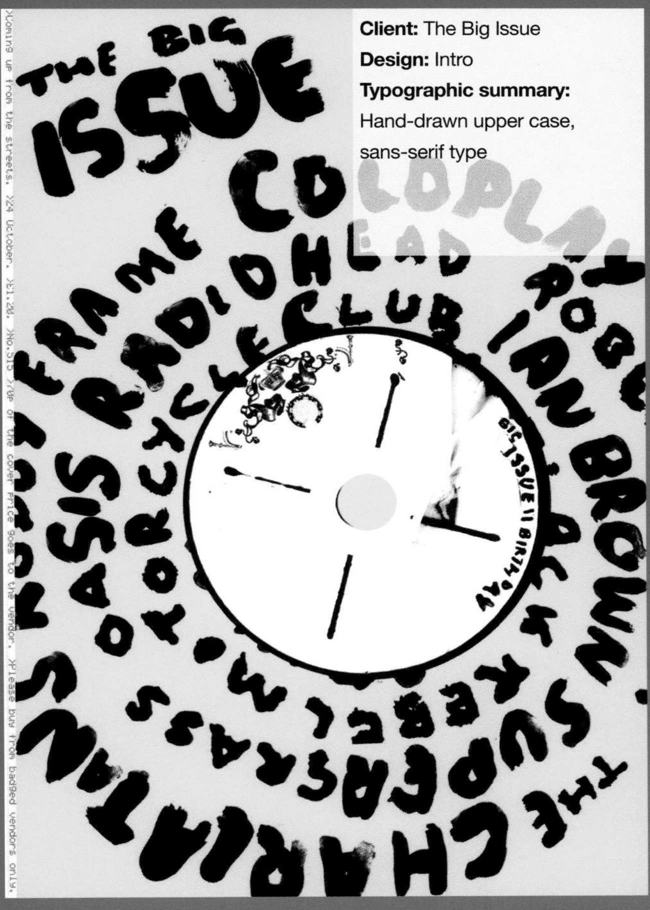

Client: The Big Issue
Design: Intro
Typographic summary: Hand-drawn upper case, sans-serif type

The Big Issue (left)

Intro used hand-drawn letterforms for the cover of this edition of *The Big Issue*. As this particular edition of the magazine was dedicated to music, the cover design depicted a central disc. Positioned around this disc were the names of all the groups featured. The upper case, hand-drawn letters are easier to read than their minuscule counterparts would have been, and are perhaps the natural choice when writing with a paintbrush. The expressive typography conveys speed and urgency, something fleeting and raw, characteristics that one could attribute to the music of the featured groups.

Titled (opposite)

This spread, designed by Mike Place and featuring a poem by Conner Kilmer, was commissioned for *Graphic Poetry*– a book that explores concrete poetry. The expressive type is characterised by a very blocky appearance, which is obtained by the absence of counters, low ascenders and an even weight balance between the stems and arms. The immediate, spontaneous feel of the type further legitimises the written content.

Expressionism

Expressive typography is mark making in its most basic form. Typically hand-drawn letters are created to convey a certain sense of style, urgency or in some other way fit with the mood of a design, as the examples shown here illustrate.

Client:

The Photographers' Gallery

Design: Spin

Typographic summary:
Large sans-serif, which overprints the images

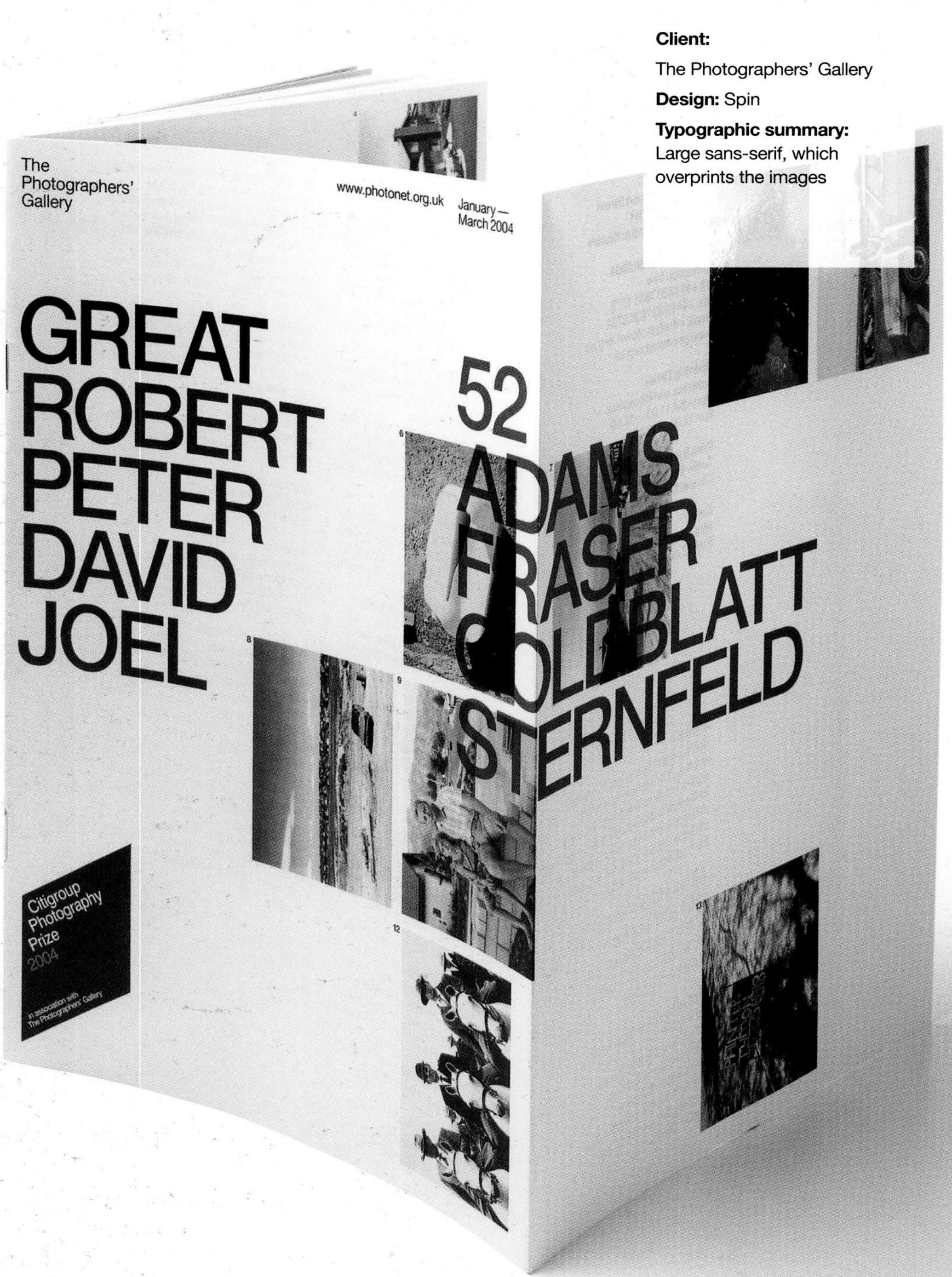

Type Realisation

Armed with a solid grasp of the typographical basics a designer can begin to use other key elements of the design process to enhance them. This section addresses type realisation and how the production specifications of a design can add additional qualities to typographical elements, such as the tactility achieved through substrate selection or printing choices.

The subtle distinctions offered by printing techniques and substrate selection can be powerful differentiators. In the following examples, the typesetting is generally restrained, and yet the work is surprisingly distinctive and imaginative. The 'realisation' of the work is as important as the typesetting and the two should actually be thought of as being inseparable.

Although the vast majority of printed pieces are examples of four-colour printing on standard paper stocks, there are many opportunities to break from the norm. Whether applying simple printing techniques, such as overprinting – shown in the example opposite – or more radical departures to a world of unusual technologies or use of different paper stocks, type realisation is the point at which a piece can truly become 'alive'.

The Photographers' Gallery (left)

This information mailer for The Photographers' Gallery uses a Gothic typeface that overprints (see page 102), the images underneath it. The images underlaying the text could impinge on readability, but the large point size of the type means this is not problematic and creates a textural quality to the piece.

Materials

The appearance of a design will largely depend upon the substrate on which it is placed. Different paper stocks will absorb different amounts of ink, and have different gloss and reflective qualities. Equally, paper may not even be the substrate selected by a designer, as a variety of different surfaces will take some form of printed image.

The glossary at the back of this book prints on a kraft stock. Although this stock produces a cruder print and is not suitable for reproducing colour, it does possess aesthetic and tactile qualities. Stock changes are frequently used to divide complex publications into manageable sections, or to distinguish different elements.

The examples that follow show some of the effects that can be achieved by the use of non-paper stocks.

Client: EMI
Design: SEA Design
Typography summary:
Type embossed on to a flock substrate

EMI

This cover for an annual report for music company EMI was created by SEA Design studio. The cover's solitary feature is the word music, which is embossed on to the flock substrate to provide a two-tone effect with depth and texture.

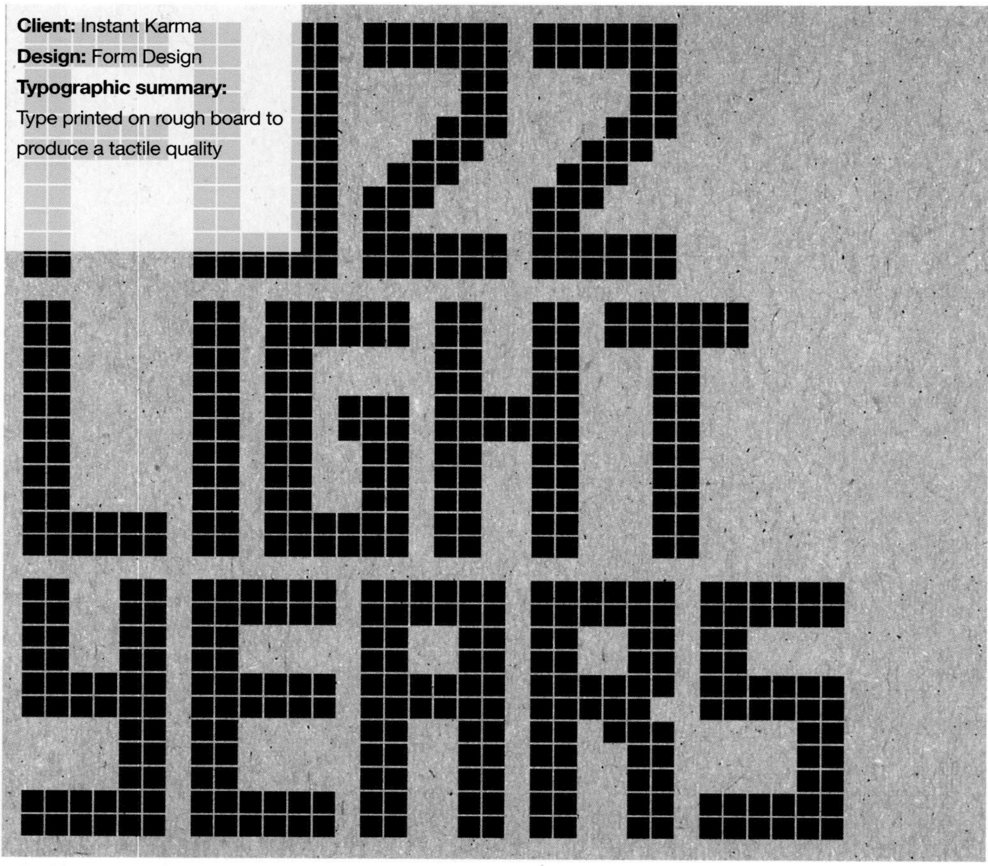

Client: Instant Karma
Design: Form Design
Typographic summary:
Type printed on rough board to produce a tactile quality
122
LIGHT
YEARS

Girl Song Promo (above)

This CD cover design was created by Form Design on behalf of Instant Karma. The type was printed on a rough board to add a tactile quality to the cover. Here, a specific paper stock is used to distinguish this particular CD, from a myriad of others in a highly saturated market. The graphic, bitmap typeface is also softened by the material.

1Hundred (right)

As part of a marketing campaign, clothing store Topman mailed clam boxes that contained a motion card and a concertina instruction booklet to 100 fashion movers and shakers (including DJs, models and club owners), all of whom the chain wanted to endorse its clothes. The personalised card had a lenticular of the recipient's name, ensuring that each card was unique, and provided a response to the 'Don't you know who I am?' question posed and also printed as a lenticular on the card.

READ THIS BEFORE USING THAT

Client: Topman
Design: The Kitchen
Typographic summary: Upper case Helvetica Neue and Hoefler Text, printed as a lenticular on a motion card

Remember to show your Topman thundred Card, accompanied by any form of photo i-d to a member of Topman staff who will be available to help. For a more pleasurable shopping experience, our team of Trend Advisors can be on hand to assist with anything from locating the right sizes to giving advice on current style trends. If it's a suit you're after, Topman now has Smart Advisors specifically trained to find the right cut and fit for you. There are also VIP changing rooms, complimentary refreshments and even a speed payment service.

To make an appointment with one of our Trend or Smart Advisors, please call 020 7323 0328.

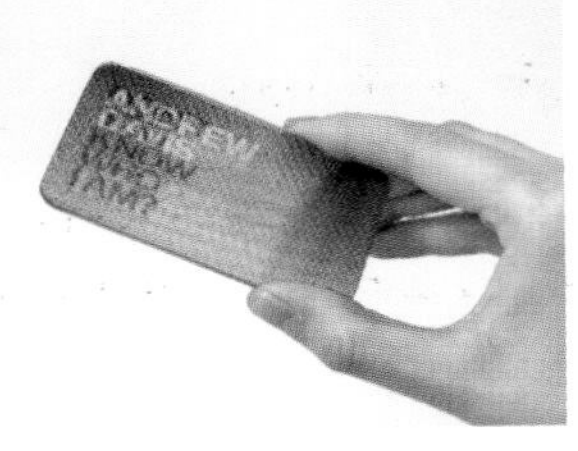

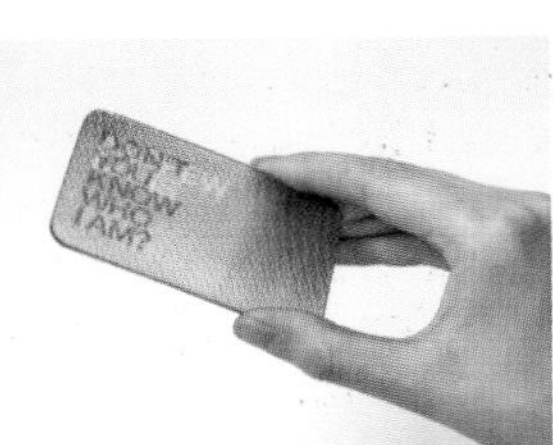

Motion Cards

A motion card displays depth or motion to a printed image as the viewing angle changes. The lenticular printing technique alternates strips of several images on to the back of a transparent plastic sheet, which contains a series of curved ridges (called lenticules). The strips are aligned so all that those forming a specific image are refracted to the same point.

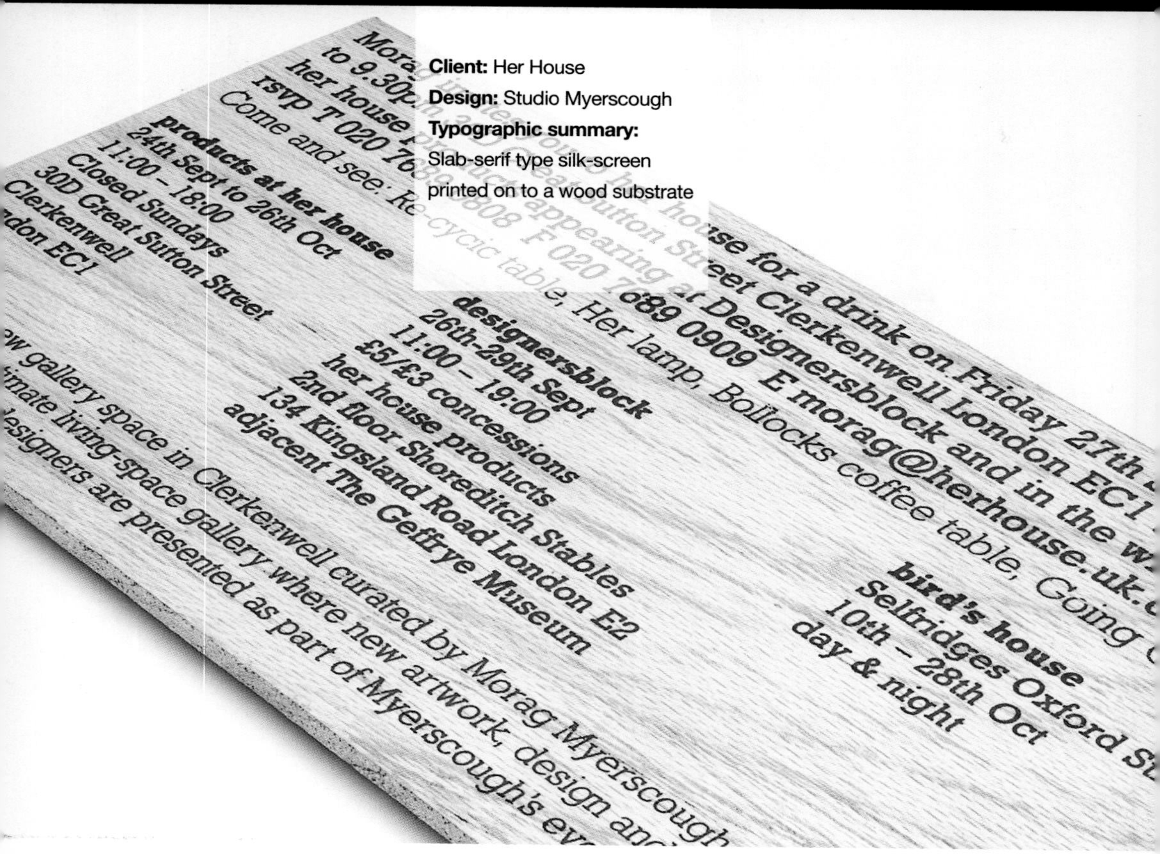

Client: Her House
Design: Studio Myerscough
Typographic summary:
Slab-serif type silk-screen printed on to a wood substrate

Her House (above)

This invitation created for Her House gallery by Studio Myerscough uses a slab-serif typeface that is silk-screen printed on to a wood substrate. The slab serifs have a punchiness and solidity that distinguishes the characters from the grain of the wood.

Soak (right)

Created by Iris Associates, this invitation – to a discussion evening with graphic design company SEA Design – does not, at first, appear to have any typography other than the logotype. The characters of this are fashioned from the shape of liquid droplets and are in harmony with the process of something becoming soaked.

The logotype also serves as an instruction; when the invitation is immersed in hot water, the liquid acts on the dark-blue thermographic ink – that is screen printed over the light-blue permanent ink on a rigid white PVC substrate – and reveals the details of the event. Rather cleverly 'soak' becomes 'SEA'.

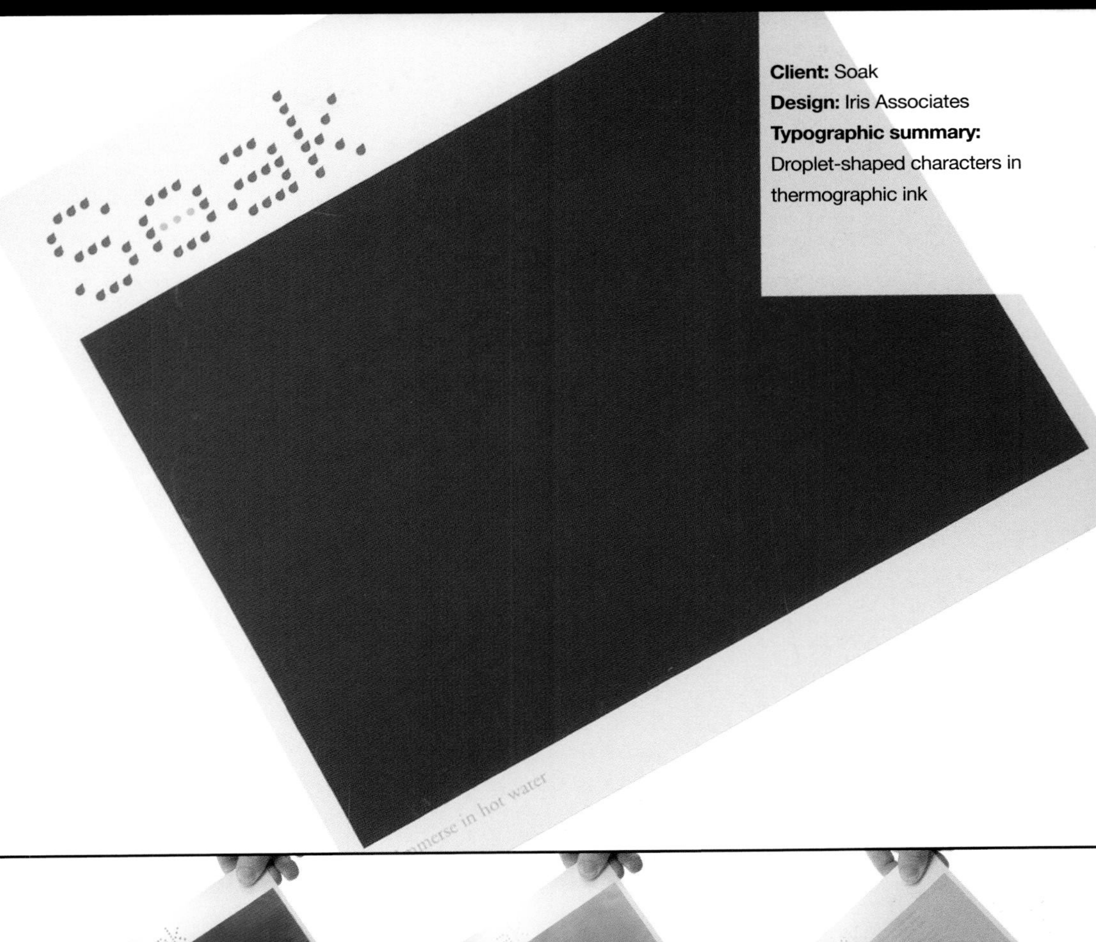

Client: Soak
Design: Iris Associates
Typographic summary: Droplet-shaped characters in thermographic ink

The invite is immersed in hot water...

...the large colour panel begins to disappear, and the blue type changes from 'Soak' to SEA' ...

...the central panel fades enough for the body text of the invitation to be clearly visible.

Substrate
A substrate is any surface, or material, that can be printed upon. This is typically some form of paper or board but can be wood (as above), plastic, cloth, metal or any surface that will take an image or text.

Printing techniques

Off-set lithography is the standard printing method used to produce paper-based publications and documents; including many of the examples shown in this book, as well as the book itself. However other printing techniques exist for getting ink – and the design – on to the substrate. These include letterpress, hot metal, silk screen and gravure.

Each of these techniques imparts qualities into a design that are far beyond simply putting the ink on the page. Differences in the pressure used to apply the ink, for example, can add individuality, uniqueness or tactility to a design. These examples of letterpress printing (below), demonstrate how unique impressions can be created due to variations in the ink transfer from letters to substrate.

Client: Royal Mail
Design: Blast (Alan Kitching)
Typographic summary:
Collage of typography printed using a letterpress technique

Royal Mail

This packaging for a set of postage stamps was designed for Royal Mail by Blast design studio. The packaging features a collage of typography by Alan Kitching, which has been printed using a letterpress technique. The collage reflects the themes for the commemorative stamps issued during the year, and the use of letterpress printing provides sturdy characters that actually appear as if they have been 'stamped' on to the substrate.

Letterpress printing

This is a method of relief printing whereby an inked, raised surface is pressed against the substrate. It was the first commercial printing method employed and is the source of many printing terms. The raised surface that makes the impression is typically made from pieces of type, but photoengraved plates can also be used.

A defect of letterpress printing is appealing to modern designers; when improperly inked patches appear in the letters and so each impression created is subtly different and the type is unique. Designers also use this method as it can add tactile qualities to a piece.

Hot-metal printing

Client: Pentagram
Design: Webb & Webb
Typographic summary:
Hot-metal printed invitation incorporating a mixture of small cap, Roman and italic variations of a serif typeface

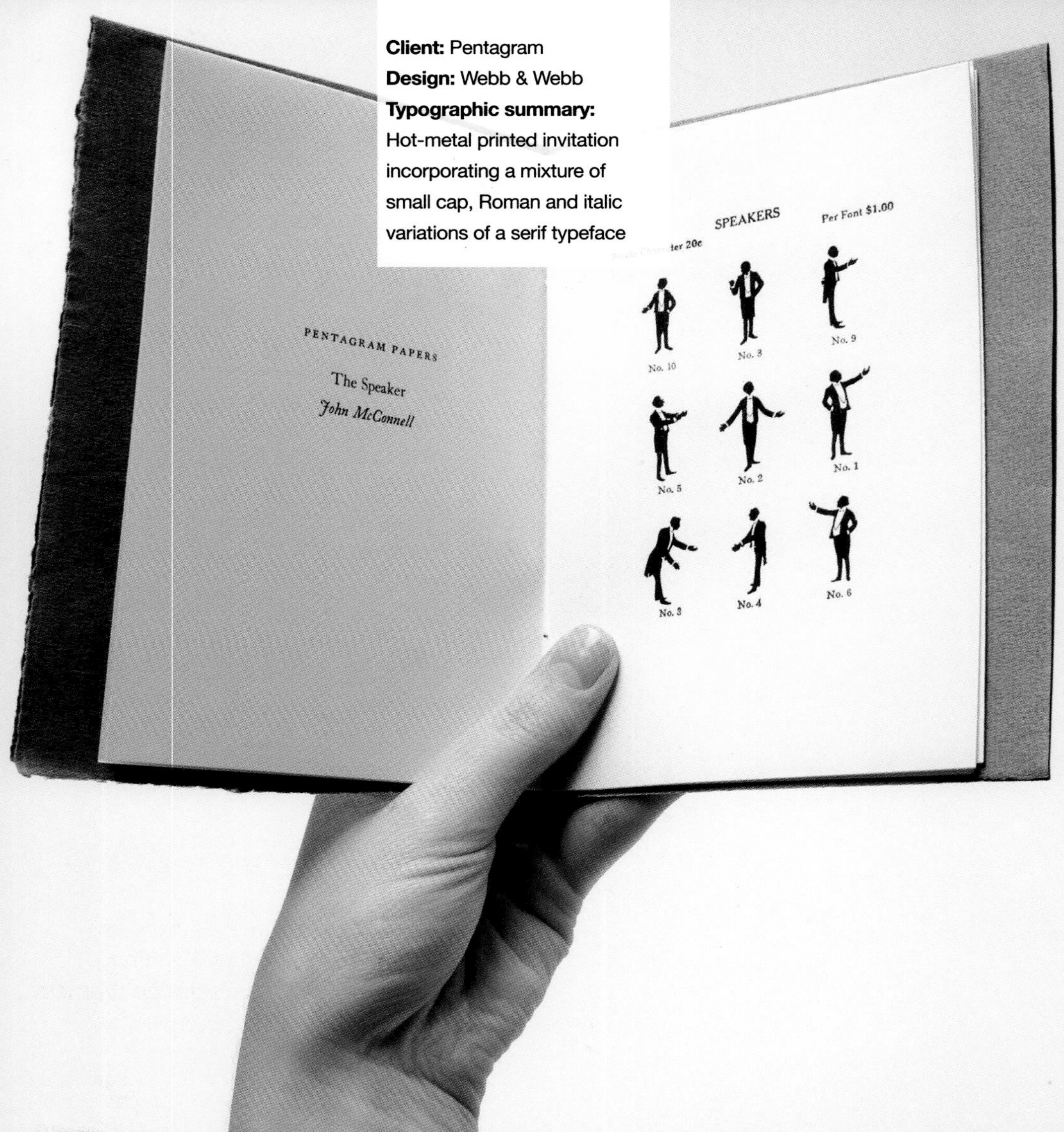

Hot-metal printing
Hot-metal printing or cast-metal composition was developed from letterpress printing and originally involved the casting of lines of type in molten metal. This made it possible to create large quantities of type in a relatively inexpensive fashion. Nowadays text is typed into a machine to produce a punched paper tape, which then controls the characters cast by a casting machine. The resulting block – with its raised letters and fine detail – can then be used to print from. The impression made, unlike lithography, is rich with texture and depth. Combined with a suitably pulpy paper stock, the results are very apparent and steeped in historical reference.

Double Crown Club Dinner

This invitation, to the London Arts Double Crown Club Dinner, was designed by Webb & Webb and is printed on a salvaged paper stock that creates the illusion of an aged document. The hot-metal printing technique used coupled with the centred typography – a mixture of Roman, italic and small capitals – completes the antiquated effect. The typography is complemented by the use of character symbols. The speaker at the event, John McConnell of Pentagram, is indicated by a speaker symbol, the members and guests are represented by a listener symbol and a symbol of a domestic represents the menu.

A Gathering of Time

This book, celebrating the work of artist Cy Twombly, was created by Bruce Mau Design for the Gagosian Gallery. It features the use of hot-metal printing to add a tactile quality to the pages.

As can be seen on the opposite page, the simplicity of the typography not only complements the understated quality of the publication, but also necessitates careful setting due to the incorporation of true italics (a), careful kerning (b) and ligatures (c).

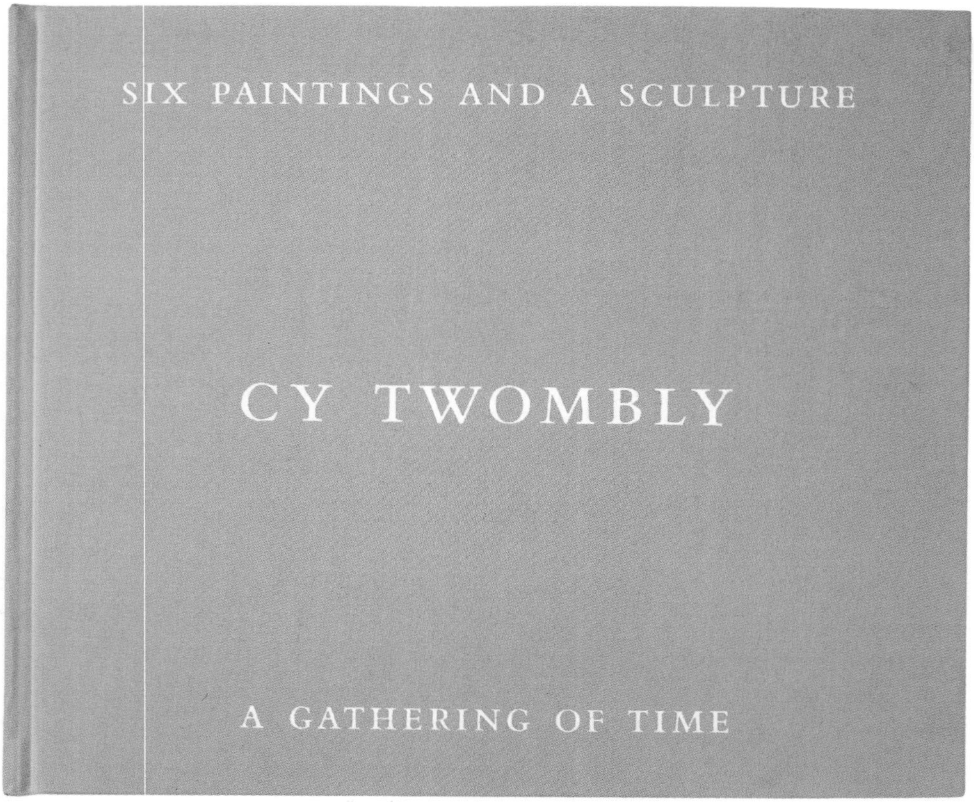

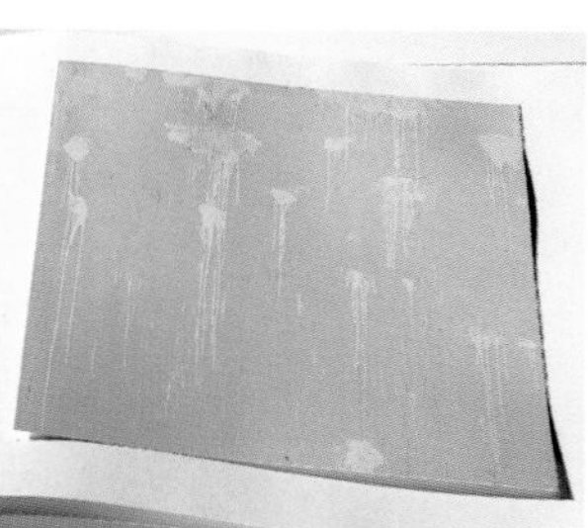

Client: Gagosian Gallery
Design: Bruce Mau Design
Typographic summary:
Hot-metal printing to achieve textural indentation

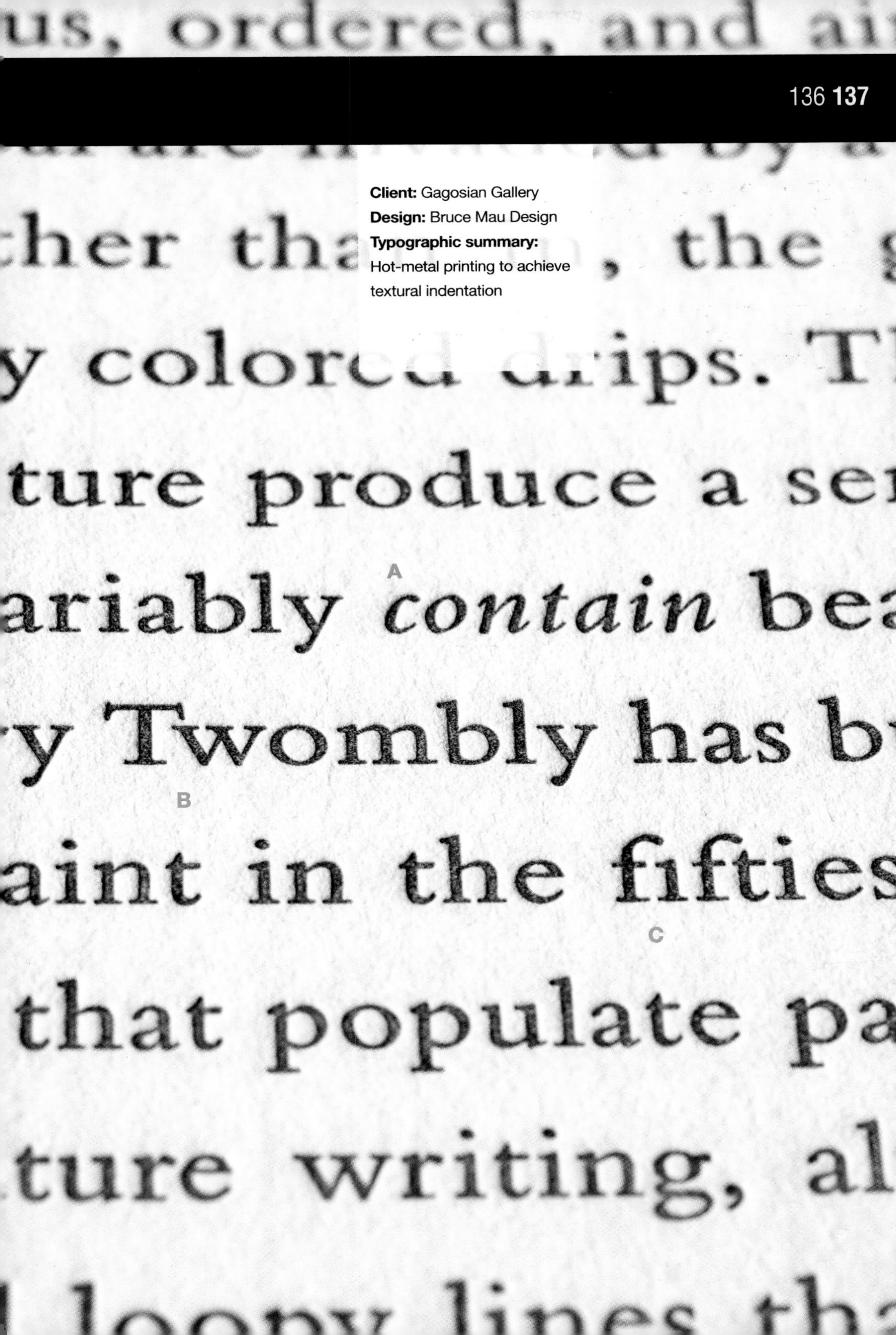

Silk-screen printing

Client: Ericsson
Design: Imagination
Typographic summary:
Silk-screen printed sans-serif Helvetica, overlayed with a fine mesh of printed lines

Silk-screen printing

Silk-screen print finishing forces ink through a stencil, pattern or template that has been produced on silk (or similar cloth), and stretched across a frame. The primary advantage of this printing method is that it can be used across a wide range of substrates, particularly those that are unsuited to other printing methods.

Making Sense of the New Economy

This invitation, for an event hosted by telecommunications company Ericsson, was designed by Imagination. The theme of the event was The New Economy and the type used on the invitation is in keeping with this.

Helvetica 65, a sans-serif typeface with a modern feel, is silk-screen printed on to a transparent acetate substrate. A fine mesh of hairlines is also printed on to the front of the invitation and accompanying material, and the type is printed in reverse on to the back of the invitation. The resulting 'layering' conveys a sense of both communication and connection with minimum effort. The controlled simplicity of the print material is further enhanced by the raised ink, which is a subtle characteristic of the silk-screen printing process.

Gravure printing

Gravure printing
Gravure or rotogravure printing is a high-volume intaglio print process in which the printing area is etched into the printing plate. Ink is then transferred from the plate to the substrate.

These examples take inspiration from original stamp designs both literal – the colours, shapes and forms – and descriptive – the 'story' and context of each design. These design 'stories' are visually enlivened through the considered use of typography:

This page
(shown from, top to bottom)
Satellite agriculture by Richard Cooke. The type is angled to align with the geometric shape made by the overhead image on the stamp.
Weaver's craft by Peter Collingwood. A tapestry of words forms a knitted pattern.
Destination Australia by Jeff Fisher. The type runs upside down and underneath the perforated centre line.
Jenner's vaccination by Peter Brookes. The displayed type forms small red 'smallpox' dots.

Opposite page
(shown from top to bottom)
City finance by Brendon Neiland. The type displayed forms a city skyline.
Strip farming by David Tress. Furrows of type are formed by the use of different shades of green and different leading values so that the lines run over one another. All lines have a wide measure, mirroring the subject.

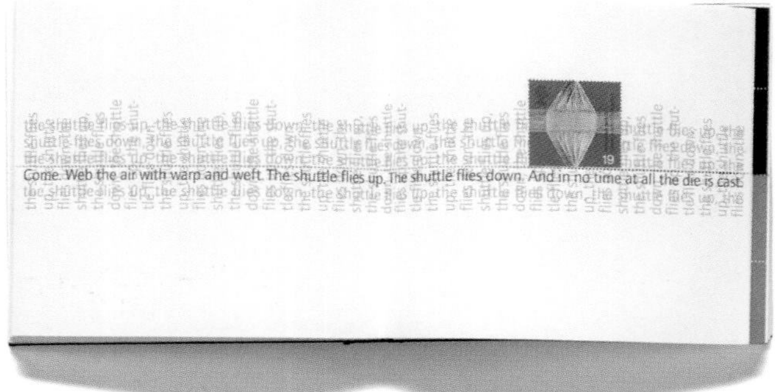

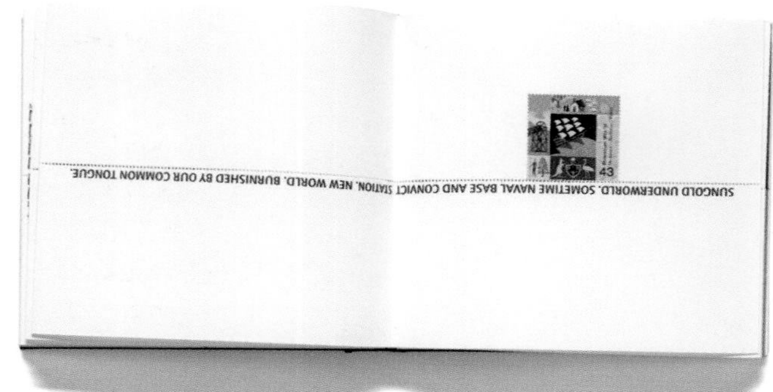

Client: Royal Mail

Design: Webb & Webb

Typographic summary: Typography that takes inspiration from a series of postage stamps

1000 years 1000 words

These examples are taken from a book produced for Royal Mail, in conjunction with Camberwell Press, and designed by Webb & Webb. The 48-page book features 48 stamps designed by leading artists and designers and specifically to celebrate the dawn of the third millennium. The book has a perforated timeline that runs through the centre of every page, which emulates the design of a sheet of stamps.

The 48 numbered stamps are printed using a combination of lithography and gravure techniques, and the text pages print litho in a series of 11 special colours.

Print finishing

A variety of print finishing techniques can be used to enhance the appearance of typography. For example, the prominence of type can be increased with the use of screen printing or coloured varnishes. Similarly the use of blind embossing, flocking or spot varnish will render typography in a more subtle light.

Having an understanding of print finishing can make the difference between an ordinary and an exceptional piece of work. The execution a final design is not only enhanced by print-finishing techniques, but it is inseparable from the process. The examples within this section all demonstrate this interrelationship.

Mies van der Rohe noted that 'God is in the detail', and this is never more apt than when examining print-finishing techniques. The examples within this section not only communicate, inform and impart information, they also entertain and excite; an embossed book demands not just to be read but also to be felt, a varnished brochure that catches the light will be displayed rather than hidden away, the curious shape of a die-cut invitation differentiates it sufficiently enough for it to be read immediately. These items are engineered to elicit a specific response and the selected print-finishing technique forms a vital part of that process.

Boldly-Go Invitation

This invitation, for an event hosted by human resources company Boldly Go, was designed by Howdy. Its predominant feature is the date of the event, which is die cut into a metal substrate. The use of a stencil typeface means that the counters in the zeros remain intact and do not leave any gaping holes. The organisation's website address of the company was etched into the metal using a lower case Gothic typeface.

Client: Boldly Go

Design: Howdy

Typographic summary:
Die-cut stencil typeface, coupled with an etched Gothic typeface

Die cutting

Die cutting is a print-finishing technique that uses a metal die to cut through a substrate and leave a hole or edge with a certain shape. It is commonly used to create decorative shapes – particularly in packaging materials, invites and brochures – but can also be used with typography as the example above shows.

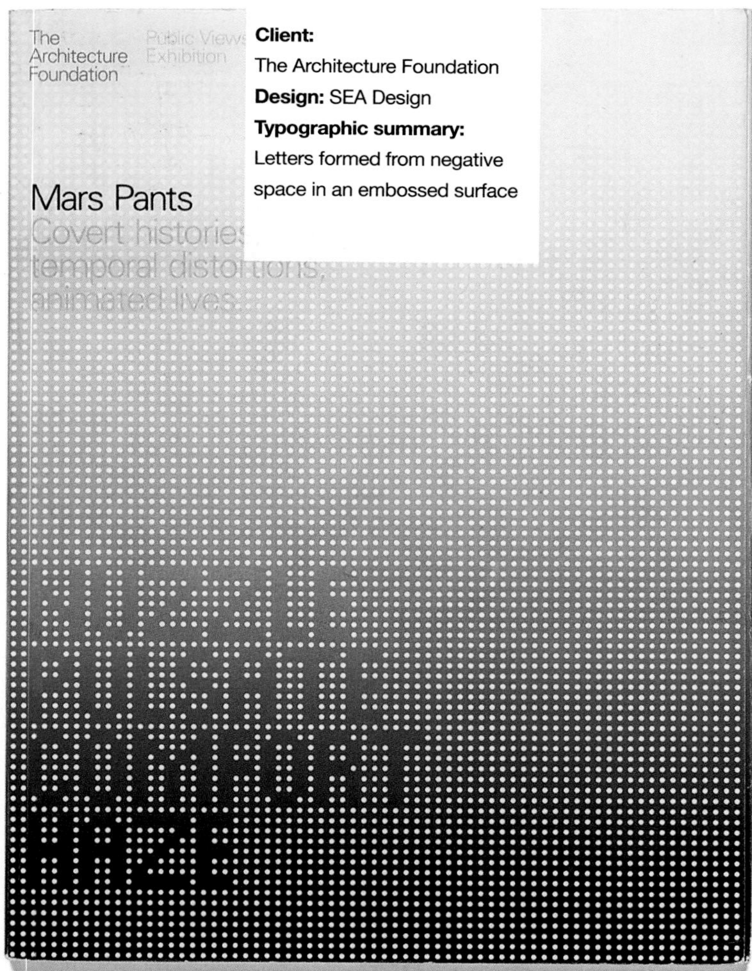

Client:
The Architecture Foundation
Design: SEA Design
Typographic summary:
Letters formed from negative space in an embossed surface

The Architecture Foundation

This brochure, for The Architecture Foundation, by SEA Design features a series of embossed circles that cover the substrate. The words 'nuzzle', 'pulsate', 'comfort' and 'haze' are formed by negative space – by those circles that were not embossed on to the substrate – and as such they appear to be raised.

Embossing and debossing

Both of these techniques are used to produce different visual and tactile qualities to a design, particularly to the covers of reports, books, invitations or other identity items. These techniques are often accompanied by substrate selections that will enhance the final result, such as a flock substrate or textured paper stock.

Client: Royal Mail
Design: Webb & Webb
Typographic summary:
Heavy debossing to harmonise sculptural theme

Royal Mail

This booklet, created for Royal Mail by Webb & Webb design studio features a series of new postage stamps created by sculptor Andy Goldsworthy. A dense substrate was chosen that would take a heavy deboss and harmonise with the sculptural theme.

Client: North
Design: North
Typographic summary:
Foil blocked, stencil-formed typography

North Mailer

This mailer was designed by North and features a stencil-formed typeface that is gold foil blocked on to a very thin substrate. According to the Chinese calendar 2004 was the year of the monkey, and as such this theme is employed in the mailer's graphics.

Foil blocking

Foil blocking is a finishing technique that applies a coloured foil to a substrate via heat transfer. It is typically used to provide gold, copper or silver colouring with a convincing metallic look. Other terms that can be applied to the same process include: foil stamping, heat (or hot), stamping, block stamping or foil embossing.

Client:
Meteorological Office
Design: Thirteen
Typographic summary:
Foil blocked stone-serif typeface and use of a 'f' and 'i' ligature

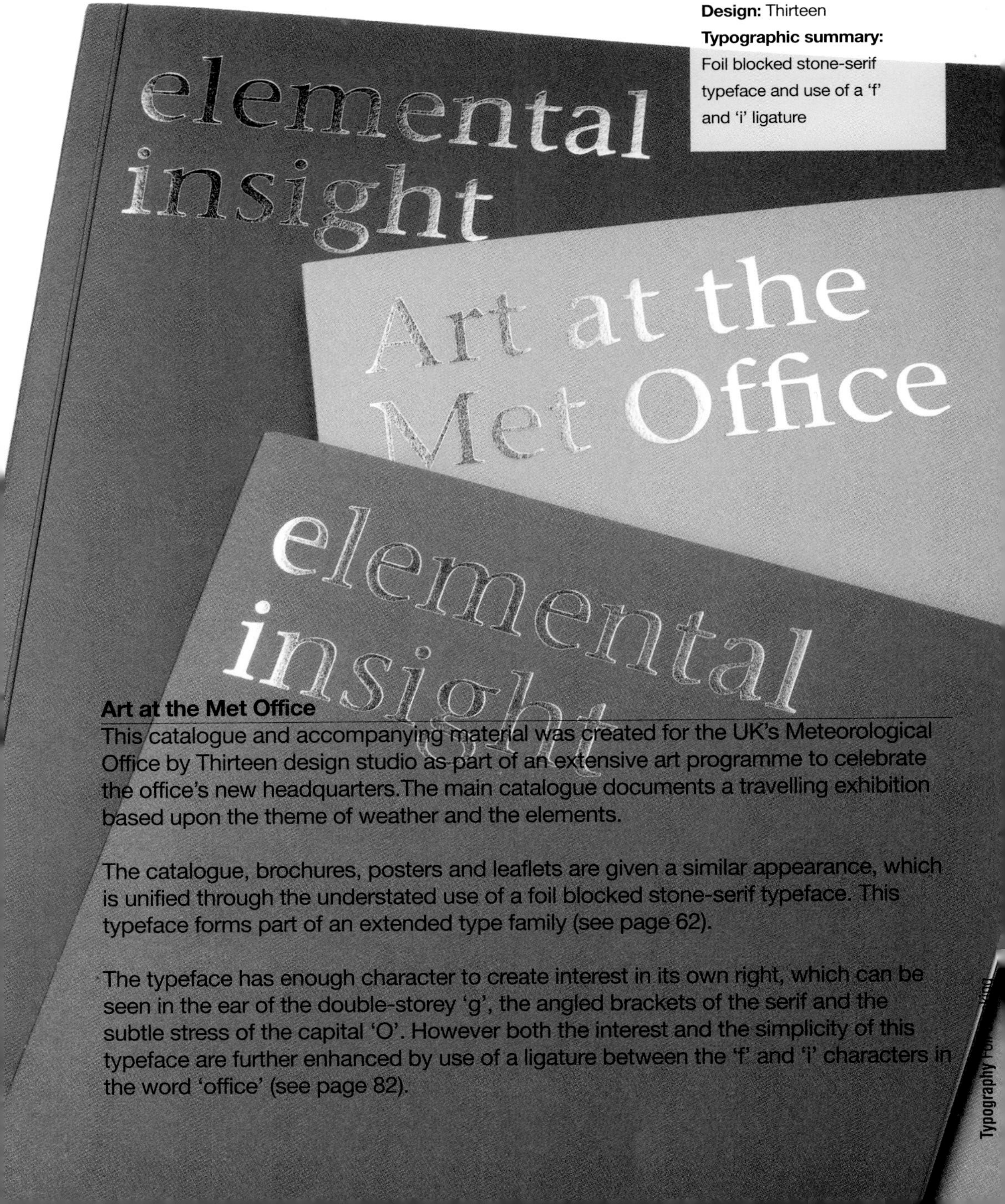

elemental insight

Art at the Met Office

elemental insight

Art at the Met Office

This catalogue and accompanying material was created for the UK's Meteorological Office by Thirteen design studio as part of an extensive art programme to celebrate the office's new headquarters.The main catalogue documents a travelling exhibition based upon the theme of weather and the elements.

The catalogue, brochures, posters and leaflets are given a similar appearance, which is unified through the understated use of a foil blocked stone-serif typeface. This typeface forms part of an extended type family (see page 62).

The typeface has enough character to create interest in its own right, which can be seen in the ear of the double-storey 'g', the angled brackets of the serif and the subtle stress of the capital 'O'. However both the interest and the simplicity of this typeface are further enhanced by use of a ligature between the 'f' and 'i' characters in the word 'office' (see page 82).

Varnishes

100% Design

This brochure, for the 100% Design 2004 exhibition, created by Blast design studio features a varnish tinted with cool-blue ink. The ghostly, stark, white photography is complemented by design keywords, which are applied in an unobtrusive spot varnish. The effect produced by the subtle tone-on-tone sans-serif upper case type is almost subliminal, and as such provides a visual reinforcement to the meanings of the different words. The lack of colour makes the spreads little more than untouched, blank canvases.

Client: 100% Design
Design: Blast
Typographic summary:
Tinted varnish applied as a spot varnish to enhance type

100% DESIGN MOSC

UNTOUCHED

PURE

Varnishes
Varnish is a liquid shellac, or plastic coating, added to a printed piece after the final ink pass in order to enhance its appearance, texture or durability by sealing the surface. It may add a glossy, satin or dull finish and it can also be tinted to add colour. Varnish can be applied either as a spot varnish or fully covering a piece.

UV varnish is a heavy, high-gloss, matt or satin varnish applied after printing and cured in an ultra-violet dryer.
Spot varnish is applied to highlight specific areas of a printed piece. It brings the colours to life, or it can be used to create subtle textures on the page. It is usually applied as a spot colour with an extra printing plate.
Machine varnish is a thin oil-based coat that is applied on a printing press, and produces a very light gloss.

Most print finishing processes are performed **offline**, after the job has been printed. All highly visible and textural varnishes need to be applied offline. However some varnishes may be applied **online** as part of the printing process, normally as an extra colour.

Client: Esther Franklin
Design: MadeThought
Typographic summary:
UV varnished applied to initials to create texture

Esther Franklin

This identity for fashion designer Esther Franklin features her initials (EF), repeated in full-coverage, UV varnish over the design. This forms a textural pattern on a heavy, matt-black stock.

Client: Lancaster City Council
Design: Why Not Associates and Gordon Young
Typographic summary: Various styles used to present poems, lyrics and expressions

Type in Practice

The practical application of typography in design isn't always what one would expect. The demands on type can be more extensive and unorthodox than we've seen in previous sections of this book, although the underlying basic principles remain the same. The application of type can be unusual – as the example opposite demonstrates – but, as with the use of type on a page, a designer must still consider typeface selection, how it is to be set, letterspacing, point size, legibility and pattern.

Typography is a technical, demanding and sometimes confusing craft that requires a great deal of care, patience and historical understanding. Ultimately, typography is an intimate and human experience – the 'typographic' pathway opposite isn't about typesetting, it's about reading, experience and inspiration.

Earlier chapters on type classification, setting, generation and realisation have offered a greater understanding of the possibilities of type in practice. The examples in this chapter are testament to the many exciting and imaginative ways that type can be used.

A Flock of Words (left)

This image shows a section of a 300-metre typographic pavement built in Morecombe, England. It was created by the Why Not Associates, in collaboration with Gordon Young, as part of an arts-based regeneration project for the town.

The path, which was opened in 2002, was built in granite, concrete, steel, brass and glass. It features poems, lyrics and traditional sayings set in different typographical styles.

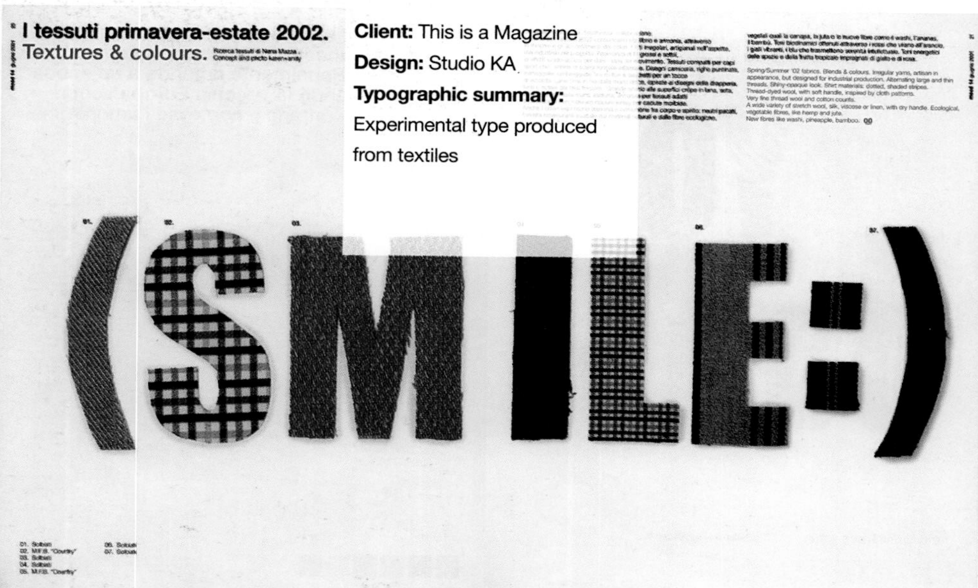
I tessuti primavera-estate 2002.
Textures & colours.
(SMILE:)

Client: This is a Magazine

Design: Studio KA

Typographic summary:

Experimental type produced from textiles

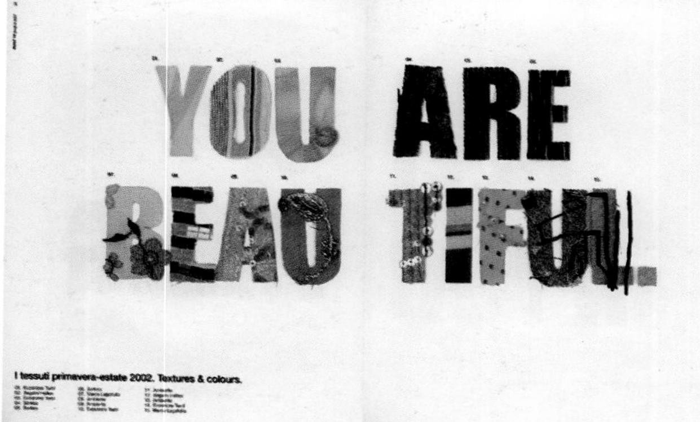
YOU ARE
BEAUTIFUL.
I tessuti primavera-estate 2002. Textures & colours.

BELIEVE
IN YOURSELF.
YOU CAN
DO ANYTHING

This is a Magazine (above)

These spreads are taken from *This is a Magazine,* they were designed by Studio KA and feature large-scale typography that is formed from a variety of textiles. The spreads present the textiles and colours of a new fashion season as a rather different type of swatch. The typography reinforces the message that ‘you can do anything’, whatever the cut of your cloth!

Client: Copy
Design: Sagmeister Inc.
Typographic summary: Hand-made sculptural typography

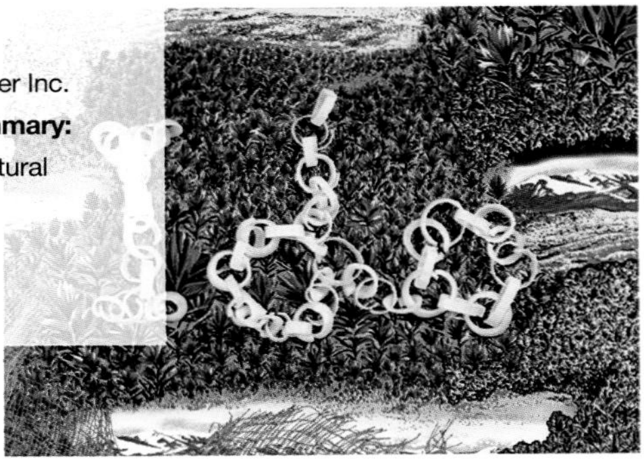

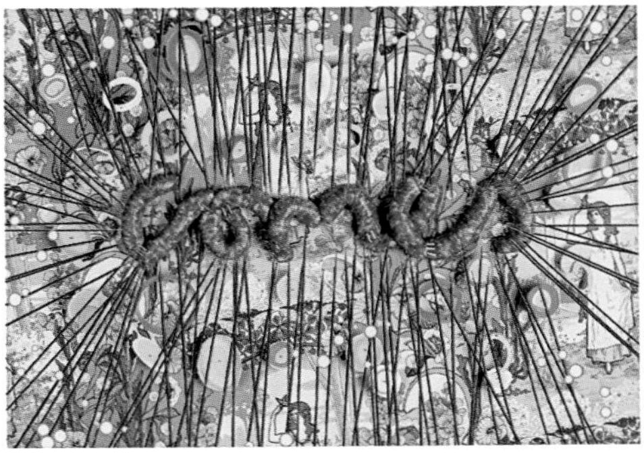

Everything I Do Always Comes Back to Me

Breaking away from traditional typographic forms by using those elements that surround our daily lives can be eye-catching and effective, as these spreads taken from Austrian publication *Copy* demonstrate. The typography is formed from models made by Eva Huekmann. These spreads were incorporated as section breaks in the magazine to open different chapters, and together they read: 'everything I do always comes back to me'. *Copy* commissions a different design studio to produce these opening spreads for each issue of the magazine.

Client: This is a Magazine

Design: Studio KA

Typographic summary:
Hand-drawn typography overlaying image

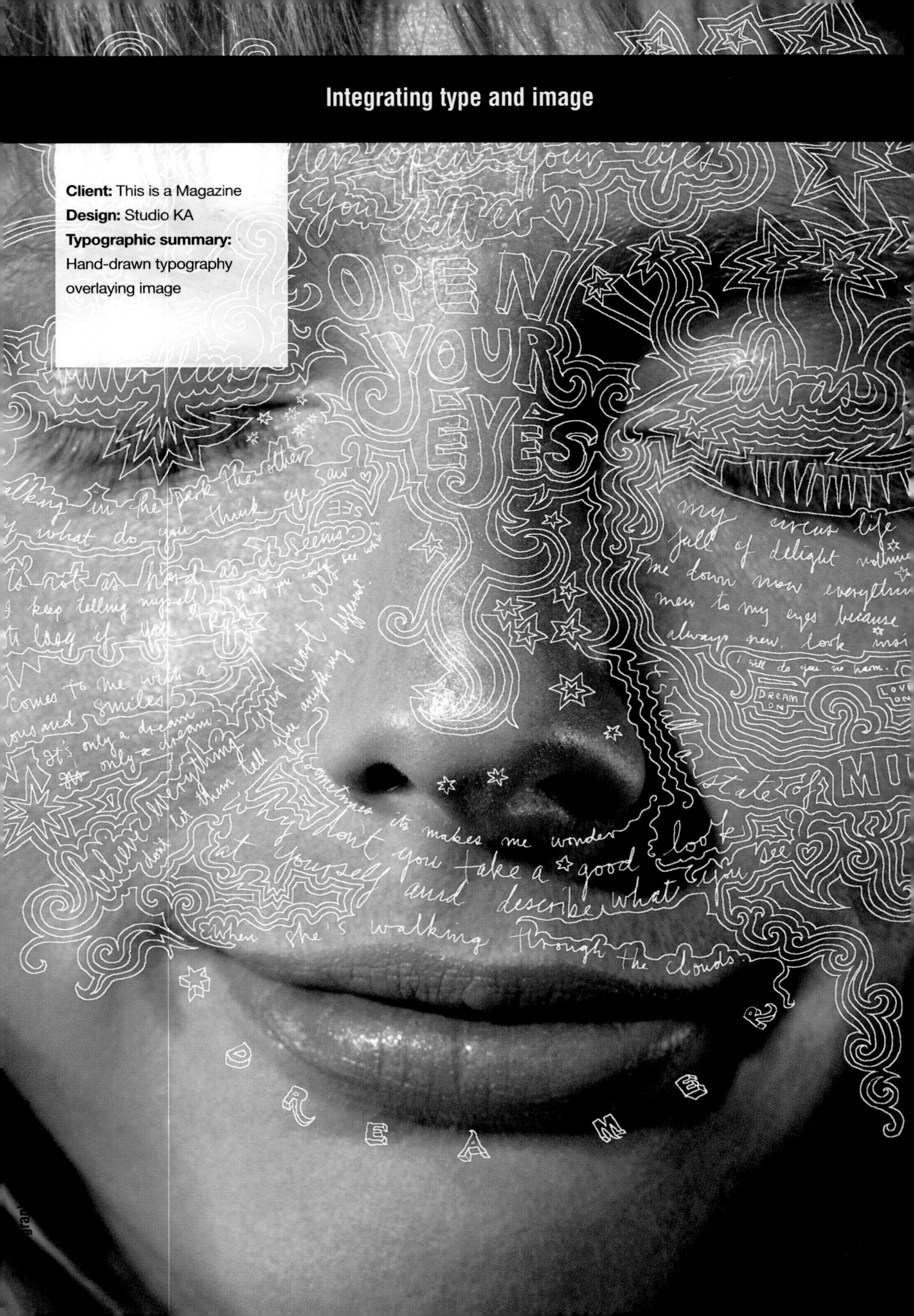

Bill Viola
Hall of Whispers

Client: Haunch of Venison

Design: Spin

Typographic summary:

Neutral FC Haas Unica Gothic typeface

For more than three decades, Bill Viola has examined grand themes and contemporary issues that we are often reluctant to address. In the process, he challenges us to recognise something about ourselves and our society. Known for installations that use video and sound to evoke spiritual and emotional realms of experience, Viola seeks to reconcile the power of video with human consciousness by combining visual, aural and temporal elements with technology as he probes the essence of being. Although based on realistic images captured by the camera, his works go beyond representation to heighten awareness of our place in the universal order.

The quest for the human consciousness is framed alternately in psychological, spiritual and personal terms. Functioning as a surrogate for the mind's eye, Viola's video explores the interaction of image and memory, the subconscious and its dreams. His installations are symbolic, emotional arenas composed of elements drawn from the everyday world. In them, elusive video/sound images assume seemingly palpable existence, while tangible elements take on psychological connotations. More often than not, they engulf the viewer in a disorienting flow of images and meanings that touch on issues of life and death and the nature of perception.

Ongoing in Viola's work is a play of opposites; between inner and outer worlds, clarity and obscurity, order and chaos, tactility and opticality, physicality and immateriality. At a time when ideologies are collapsing, technology continues to develop exponentially, and biological research brings into question just what it means today to be human, the tension between our private and public selves becomes acute. But Viola's work has a power that is unaffected and clear. Confronting his art, we may seek meaning in a world known but unseen, a place of primal recognition and poetic elusiveness.

Viola transforms the passive situation of the viewer into one of active dialogue about the very conditions of viewing. Our perception of self within the gallery space is intensified, as is our sensitivity to the temporal and physical conditions guiding our approach to the works. Time seems suspended, even purposely slowed down. One does not merely "see" Viola's works; one experiences them through one's body. They spontaneously evoke doubt and hope, anguish and ambition, a sense of loss and opportunity, memory and change. Anxiousness – the sense that things are not right but still engage us subliminally – is a seething undercurrent. The emotional charge of materials, our personal relationship to experience, and the desire to address alienating cultural separations are the challenge. At issue are a set of deep oppositions between the private and the public, between the self and the world at large, between hidden obsessions and our daily passage with one another.

Hall of Whispers was created for and first shown at the 1995 Venice Biennale as a part of Viola's *Buried Secrets* exhibition in the American Pavilion, as organised by the Arizona State University Art Museum. The exhibition title was inspired by the thirteenth-century Persian poet Rumi, who wrote, "When seeds are buried in the dark earth their inward secrets become the flourishing garden." That passage prompted Viola to reflect on the hidden sources of being wherein each individual's true spiritual nature is formed.

Upon entering *Hall of Whispers* you experience the nightmarish sensation of being plunged into darkness. A potent symbol crossing cultural and historical boundaries, darkness denotes the primal void where existence both begins and ends. The black room evokes an internal space as well, transporting the viewer from ordinary, waking reality to the world of mind and emotions. What emerges are two rows of video projections, four on one side, six on the other, through which the viewer must pass. The life size projections approximate grainy black-and-white television images. Each of the disembodied men and women face the viewer with eyes closed, their mouths tightly bound and gagged. They are straining to speak, trying to tell us their forced secrets, perhaps enjoining us to keep silent. The muffled voices are incomprehensible, mingling in a low jumble of sound. Having to break through this "information barrier" in order to gain access to the interior enhances one's awareness of how separate are the spheres of political and social reality on the one hand and one's inner life on the other. Still, the babbling heads physically engage us, reminding us to what extent our perceived reality depends on our vantage point and the demands placed daily on our minds and carcasses.

Viola knowingly utilises the aesthetic commandments that have practically become mantras of postmodernity: to undermine, destabilise and transgress. Language and symbolic memory are the tools that allow us to be aware of being conscious, and therefore circumscribe our understanding of art. Yet language is also the primordial word become flesh, the flexible skin of the mind, flayed, tanned and draped onto the armature of syntax. Here, the word functions as a shock, a register of pure emotion, an aggression that is both auditory and mental.

Susie Kalil

Excerpted from: *Bill Viola: Buried Secrets/Vergrabene Geheimnisse.* Marilyn A. Zeitlin ed. Tempe: Arizona State University Art Museum, and Hannover, Germany: Kestner-Gesellschaft, 1995.

Butterflies and Zebras (left)

This image, created by Studio KA for *This is a Magazine,* features hand-drawn letters and lines that overlay an image of a woman's face. The type follows the contours of the face and provides a personal and intimate message that is perhaps about, or from, the woman in the picture.

Bill Viola – Hall of Whispers Literature (above)

This design, created by Spin design studio for a Haunch of Venison exhibition, uses two very distinctive typographical styles. The typeset FC Haas Unica sans-serif conveys a neutral, non-emotive feel, and offsets the accompanying stark photographs of a gagged man and woman. Hand-drawn type is also used which blurs the distinction between type and image.

FC Haas Unica has rounded upper case and compact lower case letterforms. Key distinguishing points include the arms of the 'K' and 'k' characters that meet at the stem, and a single-storey 'g'.

Client:
Hans Brinker Budget Hotel
Design: KesselsKramer
Typographic summary:
Slab-serif typeface, sewn in cross-stitch on to the substrate

Just Like Home

This brochure, designed by KesselsKramer for Amsterdam's Hans Brinker Budget Hotel, features a cover with type that has been sewn on to the substrate in red and black thread. This stylistic feature is repeated inside the brochure as the type is set within cross-stitched borders.

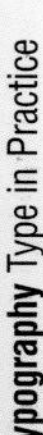

The Fabric of Fashion

The Fabric of Fashion exhibition was organised by The British Council (Arts), to explore those areas of the clothing industry where the large-scale printing process of textile design meets the physical, hands-on process of fashion design. This poster brings together print and weave to reflect the theme of the exhibition. The type was sewn on to the poster before it was sent to print, and as such it alludes to the process of weaving. The photograph by Michael Danner was printed in flat colours, which points to the printing processes used by textile designers and manufacturers.

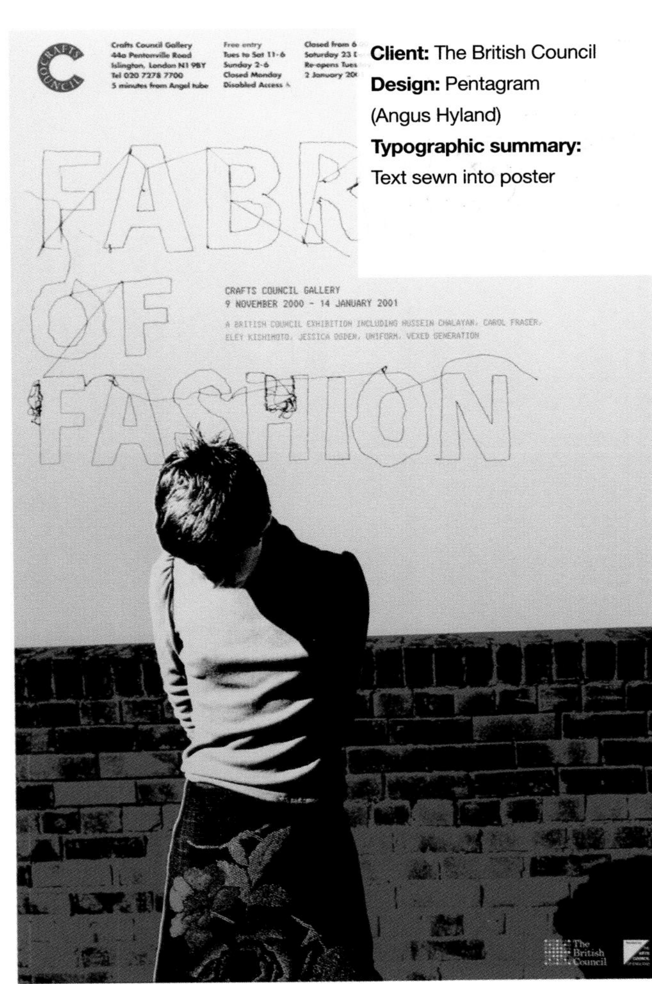

Client: The British Council
Design: Pentagram (Angus Hyland)
Typographic summary: Text sewn into poster

Client: SEA Design,
Hawkins \ Brown & Peter Kirby
Design: SEA Design
Typographic summary:
Record of found typography

House Home

We are accustomed to seeing type in publications, but we also see it in the environment around us. These images are taken from a book produced by SEA Design – in collaboration with architects Hawkins \ Brown and photographer Peter Kirby – to accompany an exhibition at London's SEA Gallery, which formed part of the Clerkenwell Architecture Bianale. The book contains a series of photographs in which the word 'house' appears in a variety of locations. As such it documents a use of typography in the environment that people often overlook. The final spread lists the names and locations of the houses featured.

Client: Levi's
Design: The Kitchen
Typographic summary: Marquee display panel, constrained typography

Levi's

Another example of integrating type into a specific environment is this window display. Created for Levi's by The Kitchen design studio it is an adaptation of electronic marquee message system. Due to the physical presentation constraints of the LED display panel, the typography has to be constrained and so is formed by a limited series of squares. As the words track across the panel, they possess an eye-catching vibrancy that is accentuated by the high-visibility red-on-black colour scheme, and this more than compensates for the typographical constraint.

Glossary

The subject of typography contains many technical terms and synonyms that can be confusing and a little overwhelming. This glossary defines some of the more common terminology in usage in order to facilitate a better understanding and appreciation of the subject, although it is far from exhaustive.

The following 16-page section, which is printed on an uncoated kraft paper stock, also provides some examples of the many typefaces that are available to the designer.

A final note is that Pantone Metallic 872 was used as a special colour on pages 114, 115, 118, 119, 122, 123, 126 and 127.

ABCDEFGHIJKLMNOPQRSTUVWXYZ
abcdefghijklmnopqrstuvwxyz
1234567890

ABCDEFGHIJKLMNOPQRSTUVWXYZ
ABCDEFGHIJKLMNOPQRSTUVWXYZ
1234567890

ABCDEFGHIJKLMNOPQRSTUVWXYZ
abcdefghijklmnopqrstuvwxyz
1234567890

Aldus – Small Caps and Italic Old Style Numerals Variations

The Aldus typeface family was designed by typographer Hermann Zapf in 1954 for David Stempel. Named after Aldus Manutius, a 15th century Venetian printer and publisher, this typeface was originally intended to be the book, or text, weight for Zapf's Palatino typeface family, but was instead released under the name Aldus. Aldus is lighter and narrower than Palatino, which makes it a good choice for body text usage.

Apex
The point formed at the top of a character such as 'A' where the left and right strokes meet.

Arm
See Bar.

Ascender
See Extender.

Bar
The horizontal stroke on characters 'A', 'H', 'T', 'e', 'f' 't'. Sometimes called a crossbar on 'A' and 'H' or an arm on the 'F', 'T', 'E' and 'K' upstroke.

Baseline
The baseline is an imaginary line upon which a line of text sits, and is the point from which other elements of type are measured, including x-height and leading.

Bezier curve
A curve created by two terminal points and two or more control points for a letter shape.

Bicapitalisation
Non-standard capitalisation where compound words or phrases that are joined without spacing are capitalised.

Bitmap
An image that is composed of dots.

Blackletter
A typeface based on the ornate writing prevalent during the Middle Ages. Also called Block, Gothic, Old English, Black or Broken.

Body text
Body text (or copy), is the text that forms the main part of a work. It is usually between 8 and 14 points in size.

ABCDEFGHIJKLMNOPQRSTUVWXYZ
abcdefghijklmnopqrstuvwxyz
1234567890

ABCDEFGHIJKLMNOPQRSTUVWXYZ
abcdefghijklmnopqrstuvwxyz
1234567890

ABCDEFGHIJKLMNOPQRSTUVWXYZ
abcdefghijklmnopqrstuvwxyz
1234567890

Cheltenham – Roman, Bold Head and Extra Condensed Variations

The current Cheltenham typeface family was designed by Tony Stan and is based on an original design by architect Bertram Goodhue. Goodhue's design was subsequently expanded by Morris Fuller Benton and finally completed by Stan in 1975. This version of Cheltenham is characterised by a larger x-height and improved italic details and is considered a modern typeface with classic attributes.

Bold
A version of the Roman cut with a wider stroke. Also called medium, semi-bold, black, super or poster.

Boldface type
A thick, heavy variety of type used to give emphasis.

Bowl
The stroke that surrounds and contains the counter.

Bracket
The curved portion of a serif that connects it to the stroke.

Camel case
See bicapitalisation

Character
An individual element of type such as a letter or punctuation mark.

Chin
The terminal angled part of the 'G'

Condensed
A narrower version of the Roman cut.

Counter
The empty space inside the body stroke, which is surrounded by the bowl.

Cross stroke
A horizontal stroke that crosses over the stem.

Crossbar
See Bar.

Crotch
Where the leg and arm of the 'K' and 'k' meet.

Debossing
A design stamped without ink or foil giving a recessed surface.

Descender
See Extender.

ABCDEFGHIJKLMNOPQRSTUVWXYZ
abcdefghijklmnopqrstuvwxyz
1234567890

ABCDEFGHIJKLMNOPQRSTUVWXYZ
abcdefghijklmnopqrstuvwxyz
1234567890

ABCDEFGHIJKLMNOPQRSTUVWXYZ
abcdefghijklmnopqrstuvwxyz
1234567890

Eras – Book, Demi and Ultra Variations

The Eras typeface family was designed by French designers Albert Boton and Albert Hollenstein in 1976. It is a typical sans-serif and is distinguished by an unusual, barely perceptible forward slant and subtle stroke-weight variations. It is open and airy, and references Greek stone-cut lapidary letters and Roman capitals.

Die cut
Special shapes cut into a substrate by a steel die.

Display type
Large and/or distinctive type intended to attract the eye, and specifically cut to be viewed from a distance.

Down stroke
The heavy stroke in a type character.

Drop capital
An upper case letter that is set in a larger point size and aligned with the top of the first line.

Ear
Decorative flourish on the upper right side of the 'g' bowl.

Em
A unit of measurement derived from the width of the square body of the cast upper case 'M'. An em equals the size of a given type, i.e. the em of 10 point type is 10 points.

Embossing
A design stamped without ink or foil giving a raised surface.

En
Unit of measurement equal to half of one em.

Extended
A wider version of the Roman cut.

Extender
The part of a letter that extends above the x-height (ascender) or that falls below the baseline (descender).

Eye
A name specifically given to the counter of an 'e'.

ABCDEFGHIJKLMNOPQRSTUVWXYZ
abcdefghijklmnopqrstuvwxyz
1234567890

ABCDEFGHIJKLMNOPQRSTUVWXYZ
abcdefghijklmnopqrstuvwxyz
1234567890

ABCDEFGHIJKLMNOPQRSTUVWXYZ
abcdefghijklmnopqrstuvwxyz
1234567890

Syntax – Roman, Bold and Ultra Black Variations

The Syntax typeface family was the product of a 1995 collaboration between Swiss typographer Hans Eduard Meier and Linotype. Their intention was to produce an extensive revision and expansion of the Syntax typeface family that Meier had originally created in 1968. Shape alterations that had been necessary for hot-metal printing and photo-typesetting machines were discarded. New weights, ranging from Light to Black, were added and further additions included the introduction of Old Style numerals, special x-height numerals, small caps, and italics.

Font
The physical attributes needed to create a typeface be it film, metal, wood or PostScript code.

Foot
The serif found at the bottom of the stem, which sits on the baseline.

Flock
A speciality cover paper produced by coating the sheet with a dyed flock powder. Originally intended to simulate tapestry and Italian velvet brocade.

Geometric
Sans-serif typefaces that are based on geometric shapes identifiable by round 'O' and 'Q' characters.

Golden section
A division in the ratio 8:13 that produces harmonious proportions.

Gothic
A typeface without serifs. Also called Sans-serif or Lineale.

Gravure
A high volume intaglio printing process in which the printing area is etched into the printing plate.

Hairline
The thinnest stroke in a typeface that has varying widths. Also refers to a 0.25pt line, which is the thinnest line that can be confidently produced by printing processes.

Hand drawn type
Typography that is hand made.

ABCDEFGHIJKLMNOPQRSTUVWXYZ
abcdefghijklmnopqrstuvwxyz
1234567890

ABCDEFGHIJKLMNOPQRSTUVWXYZ
abcdefghijklmnopqrstuvwxyz
1234567890

ABCDEFGHIJKLMNOPQRSTUVWXYZ
abcdefghijklmnopqrstuvwxyz
1234567890

Geometric – Light, Roman and Bold Variations

The Geometric typeface family is a sans-serif with spacious capitals and numerals, and full circles for the 'O', 'Q', 'G' and 'C' characters. Lower case letters are characterised by extended ascenders but truncated descenders, and a dramatically inclined 'e' counter.

Hierarchy
A logical, organised and visual guide for text headings, which indicates different levels of importance.

Hook
The serif at the top of a stem.

Ink trapping
The adjustment of areas of colour, text or shapes to account for misregistration on the printing press by overlapping them.

Intercaps
See bicapitalisation.

Italic
A version of the roman cut that angles to the right and at some point between 7–20 degrees.

Kerning
The removal of unwanted space between letters.

Kerning pairs
Letter combinations that frequently need to be kerned.

Knockout
Where an underlaying colour has a gap inserted where another colour would overprint it. The bottom colour is 'knocked out' to prevent colour mixing.

Leading
The space between lines of type measured from baseline to baseline. It is expressed in points and is a term derived from hot-metal printing when strips of lead were placed between the lines of type to provide line spacing.

ABCDEFGHIJKLMNOPQRSTUVWXYZ
abcdefghijklmnopqrstuvwxyz
1234567890

ABCDEFGHIJKLMNOPQRSTUVWXYZ
ABCDEFGHIJKLMNOPQRSTUVWXYZ
1234567890

ABCDEFGHIJKLMNOPQRSTUVWXYZ
abcdefghijklmnopqrstuvwxyz
1234567890

MetaPlus – Roman, Medium Small Caps and Bold Variations

The MetaPlus typeface family was designed in 1993 by Dutch designers Lucas de Groot and Erik Spiekermann. MetaPlus has clean and easy to read characters with Old Style numerals.

Leg
The lower, down sloping stroke of the 'K', 'k' and 'R'. Sometimes used for the tail of a 'Q'.

Legibility
The ability to distinguish one character from another due to qualities inherent in the typeface design.

Lenticular
A printed image that shows depth or motion as the viewing angle changes. Also called motion card.

Ligatures
The joining of two or three separate characters to form a single unit in order to avoid interference between certain letter combinations.

Light / thin
A version of the Roman cut with a lighter stroke.

Lining numerals
Lining numerals are figures that share the same height and rest on the baseline.

Link
The part that joins the two counters of the double-storey 'g'.

Loop
The enclosed or partially enclosed lower counter in a Roman, i.e. as seen in the double-storey 'g'. Sometimes used to describe the cursive 'p' and 'b'.

Lower case
See Minuscules.

Majuscules
Capital letters. Also called upper case letters.

ABCDEFGHIJKLMNOPQRSTUVWXYZ
abcdefghijklmnopqrstuvwxyz
1234567890

ABCDEFGHIJKLMNOPQRSTUVWXYZ
abcdefghijklmnopqrstuvwxyz
1234567890

ABCDEFGHIJKLMNOPQRSTUVWXYZ
abcdefghijklmnopqrstuvwxyz
1234567890

News Gothic – Light, Medium and Bold Variations

News Gothic is a sans-serif typeface family that was designed by Morris Fuller Benton in 1908 for American Typefounders. The bold weights were subsequently added in 1958. The upper case characters have a similar visual width to one another, while the lower case characters are compact and powerful.

Meanline
Imaginary line that runs across the top of non-ascending characters

Measure
The length of a line of text expressed in picas.

Minuscule
Characters that originally derived from Carolingian letters. Also called lower case letters.

Monospaced
Where each character occupies a space of the same width.

Oblique
A slanted version of Roman cut. Often mistakenly referred to as 'italics'.

Old Style
Old Style (or Antiqua, Ancient, Renaissance, Baroque, Venetian or Garalde), is a typeface style developed by Renaissance typographers that was based on Roman inscriptions. Old Style was created to replace the Blackletter type and is characterised by low stroke contrast, bracketed serifs and a left-inclining stress.

ABCDEFGHIJKLMNOPQRSTUVWXYZ
abcdefghijklmnopqrstuvwxyz
1234567890

ABCDEFGHIJKLMNOPQRSTUVWXYZ
abcdefghijklmnopqrstuvwxyz
1234567890

ABCDEFGHIJKLMNOPQRSTUVWXYZ
abcdefghijklmnopqrstuvwxyz
1234567890

Foundry Gridnik – Light, Medium and Bold Variations

Often referred to as 'the thinking man's Courier', Foundry Gridnik was designed by Jürgen Weltin for The Foundry. It is based on a 1960s design by Wim Crowel that was originally intended for use as a single weight typewriter typeface, but it was never released. The Foundry named their typeface 'Gridnik' because of Crowel's devotion to grids and systems in his work. The sans-serif characters employ angles, rather than curves, as can be seen on the 'Q' and the 'O'.

Old Style numerals
Figures that vary in height and do not sit on the same baseline.

Overprint
A process where one ink is printed over another ink.

Paths
A mathematical statement that defines a vector graphic object.

Pica
A measurement for specifying line lengths. One pica is 12 points (UK/US), or 4.22mm. There are six picas to an inch.

Point system
The measurement system for specifying typographical dimensions. The British and American point is $^1/_{72}$ of an inch. The European Didot system provides similar size values.

PostScript
A page description language used by laser printers and on-screen graphics systems.

Readability
The overall visual representation of the text narrative.

Roman
The basic letterform.

Rotogravure
See gravure.

ABCDEFGHIJKLMNOPQRSTUVWXYZ
abcdefghijklmnopqrstuvwxyz
1234567890

ABCDEFGHIJKLMNOPQRSTUVWXYZ
abcdefghijklmnopqrstuvwxyz
1234567890

ABCDEFGHIJKLMNOPQRSTUVWXYZ
abcdefghijklmnopqrstuvwxyz
1234567890

Revival – Roman, Bold and Bold Italic Variations

American Kris Holmes designed the Revival typeface family in 1982. Revival is a serif typeface and has round forms with contrasting stroke weight. The lower case 'y' and 'j' have tails with spurs, and ascenders have distinctive hooks at the top of their stems.

Sans-serif
A font without decorative serifs. Typically with little stroke thickness variation, a larger x-height and no stress in rounded strokes.

Script
A typeface designed to imitate handwriting.

Serif
A small stroke at the end of a main vertical or horizontal stroke. Also used as a classification for typefaces that contain decorative rounded, pointed, square or slab serif finishing strokes.

Shoulder or body
The arch formed on the 'h'.

Slab serif
A font with heavy, squared off finishing strokes, low contrast and few curves.

Small caps
Small caps are majuscules that are close in size to the minuscules of a given typeface. They are less domineering than regular size capitals and are used setting acronyms and common abbreviations..

Spline
The left to right curving stroke in 'S' and 's'.

ABCDEFGHIJKLMNOPQRSTUVWXYZ
abcdefghijklmnopqrstuvwxyz
1234567890

ABCDEFGHIJKLMNOPQRSTUVWXYZ
abcdefghijklmnopqrstuvwxyz
1234567890

ABCDEFGHIJKLMNOPQRSTUVWXYZ
abcdefghijklmnopqrstuvwxyz
1234567890

Melio – Regular, Bold and Bold Italic Variations

Melio is a serif typeface family that was designed by Hermann Zapf in 1952. It exhibits sturdy characters with classic and objective forms. Melio is extremely legible, which makes it suitable for use in a variety of different texts and point sizes.

Spur
The end of the curved part of 'C' or 'S'.

Stem
The main vertical or diagonal stroke of a letter.

Stock
The paper (or other substrate), to be printed upon.

Stress
The direction in which a curved stroke changes weight.

Stroke
The diagonal portion of letterforms such as 'N', 'M' or 'Y'. Stems, bars, arms, bowls etc. are collectively referred to as strokes.

Substrate
Any surface or material that is to be printed upon.

Surprint
See Overprint.

Tail
The descending stroke on 'Q', 'K' or 'R'. Descenders on 'g', 'j', 'p', 'q', and 'y' may also be called tails.

Terminal
A curve such as the tail, link, ear or loop, also called a finial. A ball terminal combines a tail dot or circular stroke with a hook at the end of a tail or arm. A beak terminal has a sharp spur at the end of an arm.

ABCDEFGHIJKLMNOPQRSTUVWXYZ
abcdefghijklmnopqrstuvwxyz
1234567890

ABCDEFGHIJKLMNOPQRSTUVWXYZ
ABCDEFGHIJKLMNOPQRSTUVWXYZ
1234567890

ABCDEFGHIJKLMNOPQRSTUVWXYZ
abcdefghijklmnopqrstuvwxyz
1234567890

Apollo – Regular, Small Caps and Semi-Bold Variations

The Apollo typeface family was designed by Adrian Frutiger in 1962 for Monotype, specifically for the photosetting process that was prevalent in the 1960s. Apollo is a serif typeface and its characters are very legible and harmonic. The Roman cut is robust enough to present a legible text on soft paper, but light enough to contrast with the semi-bold. It is suitable for both headlines and body text usage.

Text
Written or printed matter that forms the body of a publication

Tracking
The adjustable amount of space between letters.

TrueType
Fonts specified with bezier curve outlines.

Typeface
The letters, numbers and punctuation marks of a type design.

Typeface family
A series of typefaces sharing common characteristics but with different sizes and weights.

Type styles
The different visual appearances of typefaces.

Upper case
See Majuscules.

Upstroke
The finer stroke of a type character.

Varnish
The coating applied to a printed sheet for protection or appearance.

Vector graphic
A scalable object created by paths.

Vertex
The angle formed at the bottom where the left and right strokes meet such as with the 'V'.

X-height
The height of the lower case 'x' of a given typeface.

Conclusion

This book has attempted to explain and illustrate the basic principles of typography. A thorough understanding of these basics, together with knowledge of format, layout, colour and image, equips the designer with powerful tools to unleash tremendous creativity.

Design is a commercial pursuit and an application of these basic principles will help facilitate the efficient use of design time and keep costs within budget. However, inspiration remains the heart of creative activity and we hope that the examples that illustrate this volume, from many leading contemporary design studios, have inspired you. Whilst producing this book it became clear that typography holds a special appeal for many designers. The enthusiasm and understanding with which the contributors to this book have approached the subject have, in turn, helped us to provide a solid grounding in this much loved area.

The basis of typography may be pragmatic, and the mechanics of typesetting and production mathematical, but the results that can be achieved with a little creative flair do not fail to inspire. The work shown within this book is ordered, controlled and of course typeset but ultimately it has been crafted with enthusiastic pleasure, purpose and out of a need to communicate. These projects are underpinned by many of the basic principles discussed within this book, and form part of a larger, and ever evolving, narrative of type generation. The terminology and measurement systems should aid, not obscure, this craft and it is our hope that this book has given you enough understanding to appreciate typography in a more informed way.

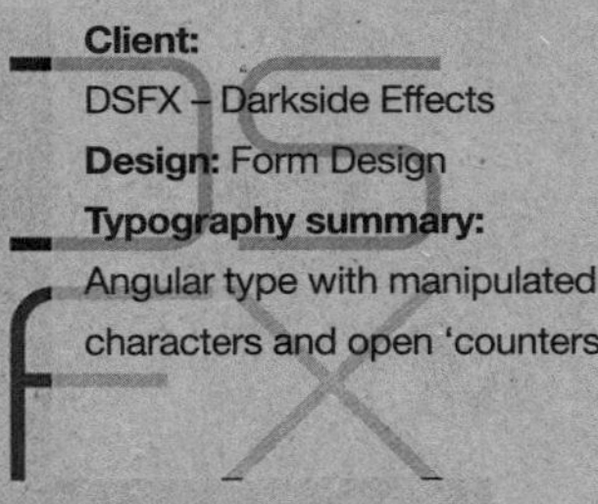

Client:
DSFX – Darkside Effects
Design: Form Design
Typography summary:
Angular type with manipulated characters and open 'counters'

DSFX – Darkside Effects

This stationery identify, for DSFX Darkside Effects by Form Design, uses very angular type and manipulated characters that have low stroke contrast. An extended arm on the 'F' and a missing stem on the 'D'. The result is a futuristic, distinctive and memorable design.

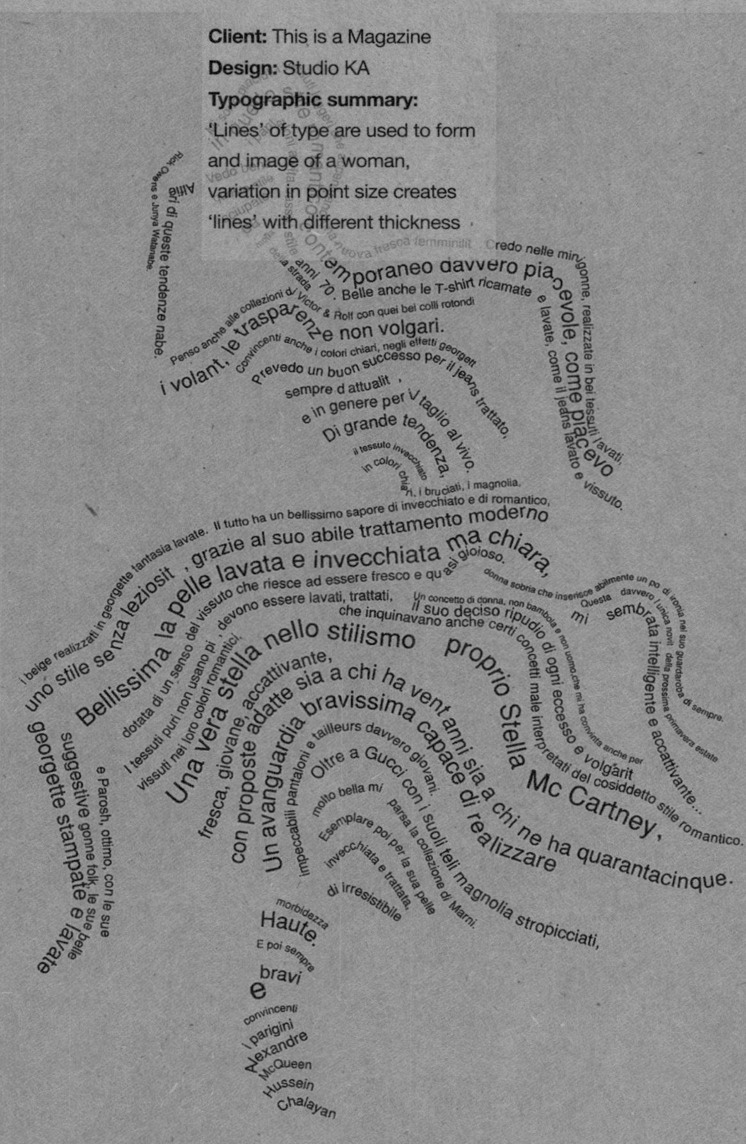

Client: This is a Magazine
Design: Studio KA
Typographic summary: 'Lines' of type are used to form and image of a woman, variation in point size creates 'lines' with different thickness

This is a Magazine

This design by Studio KA uses typography to create an image of a woman dancing. The lines of type are bent, curved and truncated to form the figure and the point size of the type also varies to create 'lines' with different thickness.

Acknowledgements

We would like to thank everyone who supported us during the project including the many art directors, designers and creatives who showed great generosity in allowing us to reproduce their work. Special thanks to everyone that hunted for, collated, compiled and rediscovered some of the fascinating work contained in this book. Thanks to Xavier Young for his patience, determination and skill in photographing the work showcased in this book and to Heather Marshall for modelling. And a final big thanks to Natalia Price-Cabrera – who devised the original concept for this book – Caroline Walmsley, Brian Morris and all the staff at AVA Publishing who never tired of our requests, enquiries and questions, and supported us throughout.

Contacts

Agency	Contact	Page number
3 Deep Design	www.3deep.com.au	101, 102–103, 108–109, 110–111, 112, 119
Aufuldish + Warinner	www.aufwar.com	79
bis	www.bisdixit.com	44–45
Blast	www.blast.co.uk	83, 133, 148
Browns	www.brownsdesign.co.uk	15, 24, 68–69, 93, 118
Bruce Mau Design	www.brucemaudesign.com	136–137
Build	www.designbybuild.com	106, 122–123
Faydherbe / De Vringer	www.ben-wout.nl	19
Form Design	www.form.uk.com	50–51, 59, 114, 128, 173
Frost Design	www.frostdesign.co.uk	85
Gavin Ambrose	www.gavinambrose.co.uk	55, 87, 89
Howdy	www.howdy-pardners.com	143
Imagination	www.imagination.com	138–139
Intro	www.introdesign.com	3, 123
Iris Associates	www.irisassociates.com	130–131
KesselsKramer	www.kesselskramer.com	31, 34–35, 156
MadeThought	www.madethought.com	149
Matt Lumby	www.mtlumby2d.com	89
NB: Studio	www.nbstudio.co.uk	32–33, 99
North	www.northdesign.co.uk	21, 53, 146
Pentagram	www.pentagram.co.uk	60–61, 73, 157
Radley Yeldar	www.ry.com	120–121
Research Studios	www.researchstudios.com	105, 114–115
SEA Design	www.seadesign.co.uk	57, 77, 127, 144, 158
Spin	www.spin.co.uk	7, 41, 67, 71, 112–113, 124–125, 155
Sagmeister Inc.	www.sagmeister.com	153
Still Waters Run Deep	www.stillwaters-rundeep.com	49
Studio KA	www.thisisamagazine.com	152, 154–155, 174
Studio Myerscough	www.studiomyerscough.co.uk	98, 117, 120, 130
The Kitchen	www.thekitchen.co.uk	107, 128–129, 159
Thirteen	www.thirteen.co.uk	25, 147
Webb & Webb	www.webbandwebb.co.uk	47, 81, 134–135, 140–141, 145
Why Not Associates	www.whynotassociates.com	10–11, 42– 43, 150–151